T0197342

Kick the Jerk out of Your Life

Don't let anyone fool you again!

Liz Aimeé Hernández

Order this book online at www.trafford.com
or email orders@trafford.com

Most Trafford titles are also available at major online book retailers.

Printed in the United States of America.

ISBN: 978-1-4669-0924-3(sc)
ISBN: 978-1-4669-0926-7(hc)
ISBN: 978-1-4669-0925-0(e)

Library of Congress Control Number: 2011963033

Trafford rev. 05/24/2012

 www.trafford.com

North America & International
toll-free: 1 888 232 4444 (USA & Canada)
phone: 250 383 6864 ♦ fax: 812 355 4082

Dedication

I dedicate this book to my sons Javier and José, with the desire that they would grow up with good values, being always men with morals and of their word. I also dedicate it to my former partners, who were one-hundred-percent jerks, who did not appreciate my qualities, and underestimated my love and dedication. I thank them because they inspired me to write this book and helped me to value and love myself more every day. Thanks to them I have discovered my strength, developed major projects, and achieved my goals.

Acknowledgment

I thank my mother for her support and help during the making of this book. Thanks to her dedication, this book is a reality.

Index

Introduction

This book does not talk about men who have taken their responsibility as parents and partners in a serious way. It does not talk about men who have loved sincerely and honestly. It does not talk about men committed to the feelings of their partners and determined not to make them suffer. It does not talk about men who cooperate and turn a relationship into a team. It does not talk about men who accept when they are wrong and do everything they can to make their relationships work. It does not talk about men who accept you as you are and value you for your feelings, not for the size of your butt or the amount in your bank account. It does not talk about hard-working men and good providers, who can separate their work from their personal life and balance the two. It does not talk about men who see their children as a blessing and get involved with them beyond a monthly alimony. It does not talk about men who are faithful and loyal, despite the pressure of their friends or the temptation of a "beauty queen." It does not talk about honest men who accept when they are in love and defend that love without hesitation. No book needs to be written for them, but for their partners, so they know how to take care of them.

We all want a man—not a perfect man, because we know they don't exist—but we do want a man with high moral values. We want a man who does not make us suffer, but makes us happy. This is not impossible, although jerks think otherwise. Even in our world there are still good men, but they are very scarce, and you have to search very closely for them. And just as my mother says, "the devil always strikes first." This book is not aimed at men, because they know very well what their role is.

Not all women are lucky enough to find a man that makes them happy; however, all of us, at some point, have run into some who have come to make us rather unhappy. These are not men: They are jerks. I must admit that I have been in love with some jerks, some bigger than others. I must also say that it took me some work and time to realize it, however, I discovered that there are many kinds of jerks in this world.

This book was thought of, written because of and dedicated exclusively to jerks. Above all, it is due to those jerks that are not easily distinguishable, because I think any woman who loves and values herself tries by all means to stay away from someone like that. Nobody wants to go stumbling and hurting herself. On the contrary, if someone desires this, she needs psychological help immediately. This book is dedicated to women who want to stop suffering and being wrong about jerks. It is aimed at women who want to heal their wounds, to find themselves, and be happy with someone who values them for what they are, that respects them in every moment and loves them unconditionally.

In this book I refer to those jerks in disguise that have their "music" inside, a pitiable look, and who play victims in pain to take advantage of our love for them. Those who know very well when and where to stage their "plays," while you are totally unaware they are doing it. I speak about that kind of professional or in-progress jerk, good-looking, with his rightful and gentle appearance, that seems to be very focused and has well-laid plans for the future. At first glance it looks like the sky opened, thought about us, and dropped us an angel. We mistakenly believe we won the jackpot, and then we fall into the trap. Perhaps you looked for him, maybe he looked for you. Who cares? What you should care about is if this guy in front of you is more than the next jerk to try to play with your feelings.

There are some signs that they show us, because being a jerk shows up, even if they try hard to hide it. What happens is we do not see the signals they send us because we are blinded by being in love. As the Shakira song says, you turn "brute, blind, deaf, clumsy, fretful and stubborn" and do not take the advice others give you to get away from jerks. People around us, not being idiotic from love, can receive signals jerks send us.

Jerks, like serial killers, have a pattern; they may have an occasional difference, but most maintain the same characteristics and behavior. We just need to keep our eyes wide open and we will be able to spot their signals. And you will say, "Yeah right, as if it were that easy to discover this." True, it is not that easy. I have fallen in love with some that I will call "one-hundred-percent jerks" and which have inspired me to write this book, to help you identify them and help you avoid the mistake of falling into their traps, as it happened to me.

Later I will show each of the definitions and characteristics of a jerk. You will be surprised at how many they have. Read them and analyze them carefully, so you are not deceived anymore. It is not necessary to end up in a therapist's office waiting to be psychoanalyzed in order to understand why this jerk did not treat you like a lady. Have you ever had to call your best friend at two in the morning so she can listen to you as you repeat the same thing over and over, drowned in tears to the point that your poor friend can barely understand you? Have you seen yourself trying to mend the broken bits that remain of what once was your heart?

I want to help you identify the jerks, get away from them and, best of all, teach you to kick them out so they don't play with you anymore.

You have not defeated me!

What a fool I have been!
I left everything to stay with you,
to fulfill hopes and dreams
you would not share with me!

What a fool I have been!
I gave everything I had and
put a halt to my dreams
to fly after yours, unfulfilled!

What a fool I have been!
I offered you all my love,
and from you, never,
nothing have I received!

What a fool I was!
What a fool I have been!
How much I believed you!
But listen very well:
You have not defeated me yet!

Liz Aimeé Hernández

Chapter 1: What is a Jerk?

When I came up with the idea to write this book, I knew exactly all the things that I disliked about my former partners. I was angry and hurt to acknowledge that someone to whom I had given all the best of me, did not value that action. These guys had fooled me and given me only crumbs of their love and time, while I had gone out of my way to make them happy. I asked myself again and again what had I done wrong and why this had happened to me. There were so many words to describe them, and yet I could not find the perfect one for the title of this book. I wanted to describe all their "qualities" in just one word, but, what word would that be? I thought I would never find it. I searched and searched . . . and finally, I found the perfect word: "Jerk".

Jerk is a short word, and it even seems insignificant, but it is very accurate; it's the perfect word! The dictionary defines the word jerk as uncouth and ordinary. Maybe you're thinking, "So? That tells me nothing!" But if you continue searching, you will find out that the dictionary gives some synonyms for jerk:

disloyal (acting without loyalty, love, faithfulness or honor.) Treacherous, with unpredictable reactions, more damaging than they seem. It describes a jerk as a scoundrel, rogue or rascal, who commits illegal acts to his advantage. It adds that a jerk is vile and despicable, and has bad habits. Evil, wicked, cunning, shrewd and difficult to govern. And the dictionary keeps saying: vile, one who does not or poorly corresponds to the confidence placed in him. He is perverse, intentionally causing damage; one who corrupts customs and the standard order of things. But above all, according to the dictionary, a jerk is a rogue, a low-life, a person of despicable and evil dealings. Perverted, of habits or sexual orientations that are considered socially disruptive and immoral. Irrational, without reason. Wild, foolish, stubborn and rude. Jerk also means vulgar, uneducated, beastly, ignorant, stupid, hard to take or annoying. Reckless, stubborn in what he does or says. A big talker, impertinent and bothersome to those who listen, who by negligence or malice tells everything he sees and hears; a braggart, bully and a liar. Unworthy, that is, below the quality and merit of someone. Rough, without doctrine or teaching. Vile, having no honor. Bummer, that talks a lot without substance, indiscreet, trickster. Villain, discourteous and rude, and many more; if I keep going this would be endless, because the word "jerk" has so many meanings and synonyms, that this book would not be enough to cover each of them. On the other hand, the dictionary does not mention that jerks are loving, discreet, loyal, faithful, honest, trustworthy and respectful men and, you know why? Because these are their antonyms, in other words, opposites of what jerks are. So, if they have so many negative features, why didn't we realize sooner what a jerk they were? This is the question that we all ask ourselves when we break up with a jerk.

The answer is that jerks do not show their tricks a *priori*, because behind their appearance of perfection there is a strategy to benefit from us. Their goal is to increase their emotional, physical, financial or professional status, even as they hide their failure in their previous romantic relationships. They also play pretend to get someone to take care of them, to serve them, and incredibly, to hide their sexual preferences, their cunning and their tricks. There are many types of benefits they can obtain by keeping up appearances. Because there are different types of jerks, the benefits they are looking for will vary, and I will show you later the different cases.

No matter what the motives of the jerks are, that does not give them the right to use us. This is why **Kick the Jerk out of Your Life** will serve you as a guide to identify them, kick them out of your life and stop them from using you again. So go ahead: Learn to kick the jerk out of your life . . . forever!

Chapter 2: The characteristics of jerks

In order to prevent something from hurting us we first need to know exactly what we are facing, as in the case of toxic substances. Toxic substances are around us, everywhere, in our home, at work, in entertainment places, etc. There are different types of toxic substances, with different brands, prices and uses, however all are extremely dangerous, so we get directions at work and other places that tell us how dangerous it is to come in contact with them. Guidelines are given for getting to know them, their characteristics, how to distinguish them, know their effects; also, how to counteract any adverse effects if we come in contact with them and how to recover in case we are intoxicated.

It's the same with jerks: They are toxic, they contaminate us, they alter our system, they poison our minds and souls. They deteriorate and greatly endanger our emotional, physical and mental health; they can even cause our death. This is why we need to know about their characteristics, in order to spot them, identify them and turn away from them. If we are already intoxicated by them, we must learn how to detoxify and not make the same mistake again.

You will be surprised to learn of the many characteristics they have!

Characteristic # 1: **As straight out of heaven!**

Characteristic # 1: **As straight out of heaven!**

Has it happened to you that when you decide you should give some time to yourself, get away from love and think in you alone, a jerk appears from who knows where? His stance, his talk and his business card are all there to impress you. He arrives, makes his appearance. You have never seen him, you did not plan to even meet him, but he arrives. Perhaps he is not your type, but you're alone and you do not like to feel that way. Perhaps you are still hurt from a past experience and want to prove to yourself that you are not the problem, that you deserve another chance. You convince yourself that you deserve to be happy. Of course, he tries to impress you all at once. He tries to draw your attention to what he is or can do with his current position, or where he works, with his car or his business card. You start to go out; he takes you to elegant restaurants or to parties with people he considers important.

It's all perfect, all at once, and you believe it. He makes you think he's all cool and emotionally, sentimentally, and physically fine. You are happy, you're impressed, and you see not even one flaw in the way he is. He is sweet and caring, he finds you beautiful, he accepts you as you are, he proclaims himself to be faithful and sincere, he gets in touch with you often, he invites you to places, he introduces you to his friends and everything goes on smoothly. Just perfect.

The issue is that you are his target, his immediate goal, and he is the "macho." He has to impress you in order to demonstrate his "manhood." He will "attack" you with everything he has. He will draw his best cards and place his best bets. You know he is not perfect and may not be your type, but he seems to be a good catch and makes you think he has everything you need. Our failure is to forget to pay attention to detail and be more skeptical. If you do not allow your emotions to control you, you will notice that his conversations are loaded with information that you don't need. It sounds like a broken record which repeats everything over and over; a hollow speech that has been practiced before with someone else. However, at that moment you don't notice it; you must have been so overwhelmed with so much of his posture and presence, with so much blah, blah, blah!!!

The jerk shows you so many attributes at once that he makes you think you're talking to a real man. Although you know that nobody is perfect, he makes every effort to show you he is perfect for you and becomes a handful of virtues. Now, you think, "There is no reason in the world why I cannot be happy with someone like him, there is no way I can be wrong this time." "He has all the qualities to become my great love, my prince charming." "What could go wrong with a man like this one?" You keep on dreaming. Ha! This is just the beginning, because this boaster in front of you is just trying to fool you and fill your head with ideas that not even he believes, in order to obtain what he wants without getting emotionally involved and then disappear from your life. This is his purpose. Beware! If you have decided to give yourself some time, do it. It is better to take things slowly. It's when we rush things, when problems begin.

We have to know well

who comes to us and

what their intentions are

before opening our hearts to a relationship

that will open a new wound.

Characteristic # 2: **Full of himself!**

Characteristic #2. **Full of himself!**

It is not difficult to know that someone who tries to convince you at once of all his "qualities" is absolutely and completely full of himself. Most, if not all of his conversations, are full of his experiences: What he believes, what he wants, what he does not like—him, him, him, him, and him. He is the artist of a near perfect monologue, and when you think you can add something to the conversation, he evades it or decides he doesn't want to keep talking. He is so full of himself that you know more information about him than he knows about you. Of course, you only know the things that are in his own interest to tell you; you will not know the most important ones, at least for now. "But he is so communicative!" you think. Everything will be fine, perfect, as long as we talk about subjects that he likes and make him feel good; subjects that do not affect his image, of course. He does not show much interest in your stuff, the things you like, your family or friends. He easily forgets what you've just said or what you said about five minutes ago. However, it is absolutely forbidden that you do that the same to him. You cannot stop listening to or showing interest in what he's talking about, or you will be seen as an inconsiderate fool or an insensitive woman, unworthy of his heart and his efforts to communicate effectively.

He knows almost nothing about you, is focused on himself, and if he knows something it's because you've told him multiple times, not because he has been really interested in finding out about it. Sometimes when you're talking he abruptly interrupts you and does not bother to apologize. But this is not acceptable when he is talking to you, because then you will be the one he cannot tell about his issues because "you never listen."

He does not know about important parts of your life. He ignores dates and events that are significant and important for you, and you may even find that he can't even spell or pronounce your full name. He does not even remember your birthday, but on the other hand you even know the size of the socks he wears.

However, he still appears as a gentle, talkative individual and shows you his best attributes. You're just starting to go out with him, so he is still keeping

18

appearances in front of you, for he doesn't want his prey—that means you—to run away. But if you are alert, self-centeredness is one of the first characteristics you will notice in a jerk.

Only the one who first loves himself

without selfishness or lies

will be able to truly love you.

Characteristic # 3: **The central axis of the "relationship!"**

Characteristic # 3: **The central axis of the "relationship!"**

It's not enough to have been approached and saturated from the beginning with all his "qualities", achievements, sacrifices, his ability to overcome difficult situations and obstacles, blah, blah, blah . . .

Even when we're dating or sharing more everyday with the jerks, their tendency is to talk about them, them, them and only them. If you look closely you'll notice that even your behavior is starting to change.

Most likely, at first you listened to him eagerly, with a lot of interest, and you tried to get into the conversation by commenting or sharing ideas. But after a while you start getting tired of the monologue. Being a jerk, he listens to you for a brief moment, and then he interrupts you to say, "Stop, I have not finished," or, "But listen to me, listen to me," which soon will make you feel uncomfortable.

What the jerk does not notice is that for over an hour and a half you have been doing just that—listening. Supposedly they do not like to talk a lot . . . no, it's true, they do not talk much, if ever, of things that involve both of you, but they do talk a lot about themselves.

They can talk for hours about what they have accomplished, what they deserve, how they are admired at work, how well they solve difficult problems and how others praise them for their "qualities." Jerks proclaim themselves, through their behavior, as the central axis of the relationship. They do not talk objectively about themselves. They don't bring up issues relating to what, as a couple, you both want or can achieve together, because in their minds there are not two, but only one: him.

"We" is not a word that exists in their vocabulary. They annihilate our interests gradually and feel superior to us, who are their partners. He will never be the lucky one to have you by his side. You are the lucky one because he has noticed you, having so many beautiful women "dying" for him.

He and all around him will be better than you. Of course he does not make that clear to you at first because he knows you will send him far away in a few minutes. Jerks show their apparent superiority when they label you as dumb or look at you strangely because you don't know what *prosciutto* is or because you have not visited a place he frequents with his club of jerks, or perhaps because you cut the meat the wrong way. His apparent superiority is one of the first characteristics you'll notice in a jerk. There is only him: First him, second him, and third and all other possible positions will be occupied by his ego.

Love only him
who has room to love you
with all his being.

Characteristic # 4: **"I'm dying to be with you . . . I just can't help to like you so much!"**

Characteristic # 4: **"I'm dying to be with you . . . I just can't help to like you so much!"**

As always, you are "the most beautiful," "the sexiest," "super smart," "sensual," "sweet," "my everything," "what I had always dreamed about", and of course, "I'm dying to be with you!" The part they do not tell you is that all this lasts only until you turn around. The same words he says to you are said to many others. You will be the most beautiful, the most gorgeous, sexiest and perfect until he has achieved his goal: getting you into bed.

A jerk feels the urge to have some kind of physical contact with you even when you feel that you should give yourself some time because you have not known him for long. You have hardly been out a couple of times and you start to feel his urge to have "something" with you. Of course by the time this is happening he has already made you believe that: "You are so beautiful that I cannot control myself," "You have so many qualities that I cannot refrain myself," "I go crazy when I'm with you," "Nobody

27

has ever made me feel like this before," and many other things that are not lies, because you really are super special, but are truths they use to fool us and leave us dazed and love-drunk. They make us believe that only they notice and that no other jerk can see these qualities in us. Obviously you are hurt, lacking love and probably haven't received this kind of praise for a long time. You think he is the only one who thinks this way, that no one else had noticed so many qualities in you. He repeats the same thing over and over again. He gets you up to the clouds, all with the goal in mind: To take you to bed. Perhaps the jerk is in those days when their "own hand treatment" is not enough!

Jerks are addicted to sex, but they don't want to have it with their partners all the time. They like chasing thrills; they like the adrenaline that comes with seductions and the discovering of "new" bodies. They love the feeling that comes from lust and the excitement of the forbidden and, of course, the sensation of feeling a "macho" when they lie to us.

Jerks give themselves enough excuses to have sex on first dates without remorse, while we feel terribly sorry for the slip. We do not want them to think that we are easy. He'll swear that he will never judge you as easy, that is, until you get out of his bed. He is not going to tell his new "sweetheart" that she is an "easy girl" because that would "take the candy away from him" before the wrapper is even off. Now, after several dates,—and listen well—expect the question: "Have you done the same in your first dates with other guys? I hope not, because men can get a bad impression of you, you know!"

And in those first dates you're the perfect woman, the one that he could never find before. He tells you how happy he feels to have met you, and makes you feel safe, beautiful, and feminine like never before. He psychologically traps you. He wraps you in his embellished words and gives you what your previous relationship might not have given you, and he knows this from your reactions and because your pain is out "in the open." He makes you feel safe, beautiful and desired, because in this way he takes you quickly to his bed and makes you believe you can trust him because he is "different."

Do not fall into this sick trap. One who really loves you will be willing to submit to your terms, or at least accept that you have the same rights as him in terms of sexual enjoyment. Do it when you want to, not when it suits him or when he feels like doing it.

Liz Aimeé Hernández

Have intimacy
only when you're sure
that you will not be a carnal object
of his desire.

Characteristic # 5: **"My love, you should change . . ." The damned comparison!**

Characteristic # 5: **"My love, you should change . . ."**
The damned comparison!

This feature of a jerk bothers me a lot. At first they come to you for your personality, your qualities and because you are a world of virtues in the form of a woman. You're the best: Funny, intelligent, beautiful, gorgeous, sexy and divine. You are what he was looking for, so much so that he says it is difficult for him to be away from you, to stop admiring or touching you. He constantly tells you how blissful he feels by your side, but then one day he seems to have fallen from his bed and hit his head very hard, and without notice he starts to see you as boring, dull, nagging, not so smart and not as beautiful as before. This is when our ordeal begins: The comparison. He begins to compare you to women he knows, and that not even in his dreams he will be able to reach or even dare to approach. In fact, these women that the jerks dream about are not out of this world. They turn out to be much ado about nothing, empty as the jerks themselves. They are fake and hollow, and never have looked at him with desire in their eyes, as he would try to make you believe. They have nothing to offer beyond sex for money or ambition. They are just a prototype of his erroneous concept of perfection.

Jerks are never satisfied, so they'll try to "improve" your image. It starts with, "Do not put on so much makeup," "Those eye shadow colors are not used these days," "Do not use so many accessories," "You should wear more demure outfits," or "You should dye your hair or change its style." They will never say directly that they want to change you, they will say they just want to help you look "better" because, according to them, "You're a diamond in the rough." With jerks, there is always "something", and so: "You should change your hair color, this one does not suit you," "You're getting chubby," "You were thinner before," "You have to do something for your face . . . I don't know, you have to get a facial." It turns out that now they are beauty professionals and we are "plain Janes".

Anyone would think that the clock struck midnight and the spell vanished before his eyes. Our beautiful princess dress faded, our beauty faded and our carriage turned into a pumpkin, like a nightmare. We have to tolerate criticism and the way they see our shortcomings every time, or rather make them up. We know that we are not perfect, but we can't let them create defects that take down our self-esteem. Wanting to be beautiful, we go through three intensive days of spa treatment, spending thousands of dollars to please them, and usually they do not pay a dime.

Jerks foolishly believe that the women they compare us to are beautiful just by the work of nature. Yeah, right! We change our make-up technique, our entire wardrobe, our hair color and the way we style it, and when we go out to meet him, the jerk finds a new defect in us.

On the other hand, we don't dare to tell him to join a gym because he looks like he's trying to steal Santa Claus's job. We never tell him that he should change his hairstyle because it does not fit him, or to please go see a dentist because every time he talks to us he kills us with his breath! We do not tell him to go to a beauty salon to have a body wax as he looks as the Grinch, and to have his skin marks and warts removed because they make him look awful. We do not make the confession that he is not by far "our type" and that we have had better suitors, with sculpted bodies and a dream face, but this is not our goal, we love him and that's all. Isn't that right?

And you ask yourself: Why, if I have dated him only for a short time, I haven't told him to get lost? Well, the reason is that at this point you are still in shock, to the extent that you do not believe what he is telling you. You think that if you indulge him in what he asks of you, he will treat you with the tenderness he did before and will tell you all those nice little things, and you will be the only one for him again. You wonder why, if you were recently the perfect woman, a diva made for him, now you have become his "*Fiona*"? You do not understand because you're still the same person that caught his attention and turned him "upside down", as he said. It is actually because our physical appearance must be flawless for us to be "loved" by jerks. And we shouldn't protest? Wrong!

Unlike the jerks, we seek to connect emotionally, more with his heart than with his body. Jerks look to connect only with our bodies. They want to show us as collector's items, flawless and unblemished, which is impossible, because not even they are perfect. You cannot expect more from someone who lives based on appearances and lies, is full of himself and lives with a huge ego. The fallacy that they would have us believe—"I'm happy the way I am," even when he weighs nearly two hundred fifty pounds—is a vile lie.

Jerks do not have the moral strength to create change inside themselves, and yet they want to create all kinds of changes in us. They demand not only physical changes, but also changes in the way we dress, talk, eat, dress and do our makeup, and in everything we are. They want to see us dress more conservative, perhaps more provocative, look taller or shorter, and they don't know what else to make up. Isn't it that they look for the demands of their friends? "You should look delicate and demure. You will not want people to think that you're out there showing everything. They might try to make a pass at you," or simply, "I do not like how you look."

Sometimes, his comments cause laughter in others as he uses you as an object of criticism. Well, if he dislikes you so much, why didn't he keep away from you from the start? The real reason is that under their armor of self-confidence, jerks hide such large uncertainties that they sometimes find them difficult to conceal. Jerks are insecure.

If he can only look at your flaws
and not at your virtues, it is time to change
your partner. There are many who are crazy
about having a date with you; you just wait and see.

Characteristic # 6: **You are his business card.**

Characteristic # 6: **You are his business card.**

It is one thing for your partner to feel pride and appreciation for who you are or what you do and to feel great pleasure in sharing how excellent you are, and another thing is that you serve as his business card. Jerks have an acute problem of double life. When he is alone with you he criticizes you, he wants to change you, he does not value you, he doesn't take care of you, he despises you and he considers you inferior to him. When he introduces you to someone else, he boasts of what you've accomplished in your professional life, of who you are, how you look, how you make love to him or how you treat him and how he made you fall in his arms.

You are his business card when your name is followed by your title, your position, all your skills, your offspring, your place of origin and many other sources of pride. Many times others have not even asked, or it's not necessary to comment. You are his business card when you see his friends and they do not remember your name, but they remember your title, your position, your skills or your offspring.

You are his business card when more than once you've heard him say, "She is (your name), owner of...the lawyer/doctor/architect," or, "She is the one drawing up designs for . . . which leads . . . program, which distributes products from . . ." or, "She is the daughter of such businessman." The list goes on and on. As if they don't believe that by our own nature we can captivate and please their coworkers, friends and relatives. Without the title, we are very little for them, which shows you that, deep down, what impressed him was what we had accomplished or what we could contribute to his fantasy life. Isn't this a projection of the desire to "climb" at the expense of the reputation of others?

Jerks are constantly trying to prove to the world that they can be qualified and that everything around them is unique. It seems flattering, but it is not. What he will never tell you is that when they can't take you out anymore and/or when your business card stops impressing them, you will become the business card he uses for reference or to write numbers on the back and collect it in his wallet.

Jerks look to support their apparent glory with the achievements of others, because when you look and scrutinize closely, their personal successes are hollow, well below what the world expects from such an individual.

The person who really loves you
will not need to show what you are
so that others will let him love you;
instead
he will love you and will let others see
how great you are.

Characteristic # 7: **Friends, friends, friends!**

Characteristic # 7: **Friends, friends, friends!**

His cronies, the jerks, are inveterate womanizers, liars, cheaters and great actors, who live double lives. Some are good-for-nothing beings, a failure in their romantic relationships, and unstable. Many of them are married, but maintain extramarital affairs for years, keeping marriages to avoid losing money or belongings, but not because they love their partners or are happy.

Birds of a feather, flock together! Don't be naïve thinking that although the friends of your jerk are the worst kind of jerks, the love of your life is a little angel. They cover each other, they call and warn each other if something happens, if you're looking for him or if you are asking questions about his old ways. They collude, make up stories, act and cover each other's backs, to the extent that you might have the other woman he's involved with in front of you and his buddy will pretend that she is with him. You call your jerk when he has gone out with his friends and he puts them on the phone for you to say "hi," not because he wants you to interact with his friends, but because he is trying to hide your call, because he is with another girl and doesn't want you to find out or doesn't want the other girl to realize she's not the only one!

His friends fill his head with absurd ideas: "You're too young to take on a responsibility like this one!" "You deserve someone better!" "Enjoy your life; do not commit yourself or take it so seriously." And suddenly you start to feel a barrage of bias, criticism and misconceptions coming from his friends. You have many qualities, but his jerk friends don't want to see them, because deep down they are upset because he found you. However, your sweet jerk cannot sense the envy in them, because for him, his friends are worthier than you.

It is obvious that his friends do not know you and are judging you. Of course! The jerk sees the criticism as a genuine concern by his friends. He does not have the courage to face them and let them know they are wrong. Your sweet jerk does not have the courage to defend you because he does not love you. When you love, you fight the odds and defend the beloved.

His friends are not your allies; they are his allies. You cannot trust them, they are all of a kind, and they are all jerks. They are the only ones that will cover up his dirty tricks in the long run. It is obvious that your jerk will protect them more than he protects you . . . even if this hurts you.

If what his friends think,

is more important to him

than what you think,

take your things and

get out of his life as soon as possible,

for you will always be

last in his life.

Characteristic # 8: **Gag law?**

Characteristic # 8: **Gag law?**

When you are faced with demands, comparisons and unexpected changes of mood without any reason, it is difficult to keep quiet. When you are faced with indifference, a bad upbringing, disrespect, and he even hangs up the phone on you, it is not so easy to stay quiet. It is perfectly normal to resort to your greatest source of comfort and support: your family and friends, just as he does, although he denies it at all costs. You try to look for guidance, support and a neutral perspective to help you see the fair side in all of this. You look for someone who can listen, because he does not. You look for someone who can value you and can remind you how much you're worth, because he does not express or show this for you.

You desperately try to ease your pain and to hear solutions and alternatives from others. You share with your friends and relatives what he says or does because you want to find out if you're the one who is wrong. You want to vent the anger that results from being treated as a fool or a worthless object that can be easily replaced. You hear the views of others, just as he does behind your back. You seek to balance your thoughts and look for support.

You want to be honest with him and look for harmony in the storm, so you tell him what others say, just as he does with you. You tell him about the conversations you have had with your loved ones, about how they believe he's treating you unfairly and that you are not getting the respect you deserve; then, your gag order is issued. Although it is preferable not to get your relatives involved, you feel the need to find support. "But why have you talked to others about our issues? I do not talk about our issues with anyone." Now he also labels us as being stupid and big-mouthed. "You just can't be told anything!" But if he doesn't talk about those things with his club of jerks, how is that they know details about the relationship and even give advice? No doubt because of his big mouth . . . Unless one of them is clairvoyant!

The reality is that jerks are anything but discreet (a defect they attribute to us), and their lives are not closed books, but they love to and it's convenient for them to apply the gag law to their partners. Which jerk finds convenient that someone talks about their dirty tricks? If we would say everything we know, they would not find more victims to use. They would be exposed, their image would be completely uncovered and their pride vilely affected. Even though they make you believe otherwise, the gag law is another strategy of control and manipulation used by jerks.

If he can talk about the relationship

and discuss what he dislikes

with his family and friends

looking for advice,

you have the same right.

Characteristic # 9: **Caught in their own sayings!**

Characteristic # 9: **Caught in their own sayings!**

Jerks hurt us even more by their worst evil: They open their mouths and they screw up. Jerks, being full of themselves, do not take into account the way they talk to you. Often motivated by what their peers think, they open their mouths only to hurt. They "scold" us as if we were little girls that need to be directed and led by the hand. They say things carelessly, in an offensive, direct and unsubtle way. Their tone when they talk to us can become rough, degrading and full of selfishness and superiority. His derogatory phrases are supported by assumptions, comparisons and the "jerk's disease." There is no tact in his remarks, and his gestures are a blast of indifference and constant contempt. As partners we should discuss what we think and communicate clearly and without reserve, without minimizing our partners. Have you heard the saying, "It's not what you say but how you say it?" It appears that the jerks have not heard it!

Jerks are quick to offend, compare and tell about intimacies, especially intimate living with their former partners. They are explicit; they talk about private and very intimate details that we do not have to know. They talk shamelessly about sexual practices, tastes, attitudes, and experiences with previous partners. Why do they do it? What is their purpose when doing this?

Without a doubt, the disclosure of intimate details makes the jerk feel superior and in control over you. Jerks give so many details that it seems that we were in the room or the same place where they had sex with their previous partners. Sometimes they want to know intimate details of our previous relationships, and after they know the facts, however scarce they may be, they counter-attack with a past experience even "more exciting" than ours. Here begins a power struggle, that originates in their minds, to prove that they are superior, that they do it better and have managed to fully satisfy all their previous partners. In the minds of jerks there is just one idea: "I am the best." In their competition to be the best, they boast, exaggerate and pretend to be happy, when they are, in fact, empty. They claim to be successful when they are defeated. They pretend to have a life they don't have. They claim to have had steamier experiences, where they have taken their former partners to utter satisfaction. All this montage is part of a relentless search to find out if he has been your best partner or experience. On the other hand, if you dare to say you haven't reached orgasm, you are labeled as frigid.

It is very obvious that the jerk is full of himself and thinks all the time about his own needs and desires. Jerks disconnect the brain and say what they should not. They do not measure what they think and say, because everything that is out of their bodies and minds, including their partners, is in fourth place or perhaps last. Remember, he, the super-egomaniac, needs to be the first in everything. Therefore, all that we are annoys them; they become dissatisfied with everything that they seemed to love. Even the way they approach us, talk about our looks, comment about our sexuality or show that something is not to their liking becomes grotesque and offensive. We turn uninteresting overnight: "yesterday's news." Jerks have a perfect synchronization between their mouths and their mess.

Living with them would be a little less miserable if they were mute. Jerks use to constantly compare us in an insensitive and rude way with their previous partners. Their comments about our personality, physical appearance, how we dress, which accessories we use, and other aspects, lack sensitiveness, and understanding. Jerks are great at offending, but under no circumstance should they feel offended by you! Incorrect approaches, attacks, humiliating or diminishing them can bury the relationship.

They do not tolerate any kind of criticism or ridicule of their belongings, family, friends, past and present situations or any decision they make. They feel untouchable and become extremely sensitive. Instead, we are ridiculed by them all the time. Any comment, however simple, though not said in reference to their person, lights their flame of anger and rebellion. All that we say (even innocently), will be censored. They do not bear or tolerate anything that threatens their "manhood." They do not tolerate comments or criticism of their way of thinking or acting. Pointing out any defects that appear to belittle or diminish in any way their former partners, even though they don't love them anymore, is unbearable. Although they denigrate their former partners to death, in their imagination, they remain "involved" with them, and everything connected with their former partners will always be better than you.

If he cannot talk to you as you deserve
he will not make you feel like you've dreamed of.
If your partner does not mince his words,
don't expect he will measure his actions.

Characteristic # 10: **We, the sensitive ones**

Characteristic # 10: **We, the sensitive ones**

Jerks suffer of the same condition that is caused by alcohol. Drunks forget all the incidents and words resulting under the influence of alcohol. When they sober up and regain their mental clarity, they realize their bad actions. They realize they have made many mistakes, but do not have the courage to face them and admit their screw-ups. Then they start projecting themselves.

Projection is the easiest way to get away with and wash away their sins. With this technique jerks come out almost unscathed and make everyone around them feel that they are wrong and that they should be more compassionate. What this achieves is that in the future they are treated with greater understanding and tolerance because they are the "victims."

It is very easy and convenient to hurt someone without apologizing and then dump all the responsibility on others. Offending is not the difficult part; the difficult part is to accept that you have offended someone and apologize . . . however this is something that jerks don't even know about. Jerks are excellent at offending, but do not have the courage to accept that they have offended and do not have the balls to say "sorry." It is easier for jerks to distort their actions and accuse us of being super sensitive, instead of apologizing.

Jerks recognize and know when they hurt, damage or make us feel uncomfortable, but they do not accept it. This is because behind their words is hidden precisely what they and their friends think. Because they are convinced of what they think, they see it as an absolute truth that needs no apology. They know when they have hurt us and have not measured their words, but show no consideration. Using this type of conduct with us becomes natural for them, a day to day behavior. In their eyes, their behavior is not bad or harmful. They consider their words as a demonstration of honesty and realism, even if they break our heart into pieces. Worse, our reactions, our blushes and tears when we are hurt or embarrassed by their cruelty, are considered ridiculous. We are seen as, ultra-sensitive silly women to which things have to be said in "baby talk". We are often told, "I just can't talk to you anymore," or, "I will not tell you anything anymore." However, it would be much more effective if jerks disconnected their "third leg" and connected their brain with their mouth before speaking. If only they would think and then speak with a more useful purpose than to criticize, mock or diminish us, their romantic relationships would be more effective and would not fail so often.

If he considers you a hypersensitive person

when he offends you, a silly when you cry,

and makes you feel guilty

because you are not happy by his side,

then it's time to look for someone who

makes every effort not to offend you,

to comfort you when you cry,

and who goes out of his way to make you happy.

Characteristic # 11: **The super "machos"!**

Characteristic # 11: **The super "machos"!**

It is necessary that in your life as a couple you both know if you are satisfied in the sexual sense. Effective and honest communication is necessary so that both of you can fully enjoy your intimate moments. Every day thousands of couples face problems in their sexual communication. Some fear being too demanding; others keep "taboos" generally learned in the family, and hide them because they think it will hurt or upset their partners. The fear of free expression of sexual desires causes sexual dissatisfaction and is the reason for many breakups in couples today. It is advisable that the couple talks often during their moments of intimacy and that they encourage one another to express what they want in a sexual communion and whether they are or not satisfied.

Jerks, as they are not interested in knowing whether you are satisfied or not, give little importance to this subject. Rather, they want their own satisfaction, and they play a good role in their "character". Even if you have not managed to reach the climax, he just wants to be satisfied and know that you will tell your friends how good he is at "doing it". And if by any chance you have had a better lover, he prefers not to know. If you have confessed to him that someone else in your past was a better lover, that person will become his worst enemy, however, when the conversation gets to this point, the jerk will prefer to change the subject. Jerks are in constant pursuit of our private information so they can surpass our past sexual experiences. Intimate moments become tense, and sex becomes a boxing ring. The jerk is not focused on how special it is to be with you; he does not enjoy your body or your touch, let alone your tenderness and love for him. He is focused on his "third leg", in that you scream loudly and often, and in you constantly telling him how great he is in bed or how good he knows how to do it.

Jerks, in their self-centered, macho world, cannot live with the doubt that we have had better lovers than them. So they constantly ask if their "little friend" is of a good size, if we are amazed and how satisfied we are. Many times they cannot even fully enjoy sex. They feel the need to be the best and leave you exhausted, as if intimacy was a world championship. Jerks do not ask about your satisfaction in order to please you. In fact their main purpose is to bolster their own ego and hear what they want to hear. In order to be "functional", they have the desire and need to know that they satisfy you in a supernatural way, and they get full of absurd jealousy if they suspect you've enjoyed "it" more with another person, rather than them.

After sleeping with us several times, jerks underestimate the importance of intimacy. Their tenderness and caresses merge into an abyss of routine and lack of foreplay or preparation for intimacy. As a song by *Ednita Nazario* songs tells, "You know, I am angry, because you turn mute when I ask for more, you arrive, "devour me" for half-an-hour and you want to leave and you turn cold and I feel weird, you're a wave that hits me all of a sudden and suddenly leaves."

This is where we get more confused. You make love with him because you love him; he makes it with you to show how "macho" he is and to reach his own sexual satisfaction. Do not look for prolonged or loving intercourse with a jerk. Sex with a jerk is short, and in his own way. No touching or kind words; it is not a gift of love. It is a service we are giving, until the jerk reaches his climax. The worst thing is that when they finish, we feel a strong desire to embrace them, to feel close to them. We want to let them know how much we love them, and that's when the jerk is more distant and thoughtful. It is as if he wanted another person there and not you. They make us feel empty, used and unable to do anything to make them happy. If he is more involved in his own satisfaction and in having you constantly telling him how well he is in bed, the relationship will not work. You will not want to spend a lifetime repeating what he wants to hear about his penis so that everything goes wonderfully!

Once again, the jerk shows how insecure he is. This same impulse is what moves them to constantly seek new thrills. The day you get tired of repeating what he wants to hear, when you do not show faces of delight for him or he does not hear you scream loud enough to wake the neighbors, he will run to find someone else that keeps his ego at the top so that his "little friend" can keep "functioning". Sex with jerks does not work based on feelings between both of you and genuine enjoyment, but on how often you tell him and show him what a "super macho" he is!

Reflect: Do you want to be with someone
that idolizes his "dick"
and that constantly needs to know if
he is man enough?
Or would you prefer someone
you know is a real man, discreet and loyal?
Remember: A real man is a man;
not a pretension of a man.

Characteristic # 12: **Are you his walking line of credit? Watch out!**

Characteristic # 12: **Are you his walking line of credit? Watch out!**

What a big contradiction! When you first met him he didn't need anything, he was stable, he appeared to be problem-free regarding his position, his car and his apartment or multiple properties, and his designer clothes were impeccable. He traveled a lot and frequented luxurious places, had a collection of watches and matchbooks from many fashionable bars and clubs on his desk. There were so many luxuries and comforts that he enjoyed, that made you look economically disadvantaged compared to everything he had and had accomplished. However, very few know that the jerk hides a life that is the opposite of what he shows to others.

The reality is that he is in bankruptcy or is on the edge of being bankrupt. His salary, however large he wants it to appear to be, vanishes in alimonies and payments of his belongings. He can barely afford his luxuries, and every time he eats at an expensive place, he has problems in his bank account. He has

71

a Mercedes-Benz and a modern mobile phone, but they are both paid by the company he works for. Creditors know him as "the lousy payer," and he pleads for payment plans at the places and dealerships who thought he was rich. While he is buying a Harley-Davidson, the electricity is being shut off at his apartment, and to have running water, he cheats the water meter. While he wears brand-name clothes and eats at expensive places, he is several months behind on the maintenance fees of his properties. He uses items that appear to be expensive, but they were really bought in Chinatown. He has to play the juggler to cover his expenses, while still talking about thousands as if they were pennies. Jerks live in a world of pretensions, and that's where they meet us. How unlucky!

Jerks are not looking for any type of woman. They look for a woman who will serve as a final piece in their appearances: A woman who bears with his nature, his lies, his unhealthy behavior and his lack of resources. He hunts for a woman to help him with his expenses and makes sacrifices so that he can pretend to live well without having to sacrifice a lot. A woman who does not flinch or discuss his financial situation with anyone, for it would be the end of his life of appearances. He desperately needs a woman who is his financial support, preferably a businesswoman, perhaps director of a major company, or successful otherwise. In this way she covers his expenses, and he pays her back with casual sex and cheating.

At first they will not ask for financial assistance, because their pride is well above this. However, since you love him, you offer to help him selflessly. Your genuine interest is his way in, just what he was looking for. You help him because you trust him and do not want to see him look bad. He makes you believe he's a victim of his ex, his children and his parents, but you will soon learn the truth.

As you help pay his bills (apartment, car, home, school for his children, his luxuries and whims), even if he has promised you to "pay you back," you see he keeps getting involved in more and more economic situations. He doesn't have enough to pay for food and other basic things he needs at home, but he buys more luxuries, knowing that he cannot pay for them. Maybe he buys a motorcycle, a speedboat or a sports car. You help with the household expenses, you help him because he is in a difficult time (bless his heart!), and then you realize he has been fooling you. Supposedly he is in a bad financial situation, but he does not stop drinking with friends or going out with other women—he always has money for that. While you pay for him, he pays for other women. He does not stop eating at expensive places, and tries to maintain a life of constant appearances.

To jerks, sometimes we are maniacs or hypersensitive, we exaggerate a lot and, well, all the negative characteristics they want to give us. However, when it comes to paying for something, they put on their incredible grieving puppy faces. They even act loving! We end up feeling so sorry for them, that we open our wallets and pay. How bad! Well, I did it because "the poor man is in a terrible financial situation." Meanwhile, the jerk in your life laughs behind your back and lives like a rich man at your expense.

Do not mistakenly think he loves you
when it is your wallet he loves.

Characteristic # 13: **Always victims**

Characteristic # 13: **Always victims**

Life with a jerk is such a paradox that it could be studied for a lifetime. They are so contradictory! At first glance, they seem as strong and invincible as steadfast columns: Fearless, competent, determined and hard to disrupt. They appear to have a distinct and solid personality, as if they were covered by a wall of unbreakable security. They show confidence when they speak and determination when they act, they win all their arguments and are really, really vain. But this security wall is nothing more than a fragile cloak or an easily torn cardboard shell.

Under the appearance of invincibility they hide many fears and worries that they are ashamed to show. They are afraid of being ridiculed or criticized. In fact, they conceal their embarrassing or painful experiences. They disguise flaws and limitations, but mainly they hide their biggest flaw—their insecurity. Chances are that if a jerk reads this he will say, "Me, insecure? You're wrong, I am quite sure of myself." I say to that jerk that he is cheating himself.

Inside, jerks are very insecure. That is why they have to use criticism, ridicule and comparison on their partners. Jerks project their shortcomings and do not accept their faults. Accepting an error or defect causes their cardboard shell to get wet and fall, leaving them naked and feeling insecure and vulnerable to others.

So then, the jerk's self-esteem depends on finding flaws in us? Absolutely, yes! Jerks look constantly for faults in their partner, and make her feel a stupid woman whom they have to teach and guide. This gives them the chance to show off like they do with everyone.

What happens when you put a diamond next to cubic zirconium? The diamond outshines the zirconium, right? The same goes for jerks: not being what they seem to be, and looking at their partners, who really are so strong, their self assurance is undermined and they need to destroy us. The more insecure, unprotected and helpless he makes you believe you are, the more he increases his own self-assurance. The lower self-esteem you have, the more his ego grows, along with his authority and his apparent strength. But the day his insecurity is discovered and his shell falls, he quickly turns to his "fairy godmother,"—the psychological game.

He will play the victim and you will be for him the evil Cruella DeVil. They are weak inside: When they make even a small mistake, they are "profiled" and collapse. They hide under the protective mantle of self-pity, proclaiming themselves the victims of their love relationships, so much so that we get to see their former partners as the incarnate devil and them, as gentle lambs, full of virtues.

So who is really weak? Is it you, "the silly one in love?" No, the weak ones are them, the jerks. If the chess game is not played to their convenience, and we make an unexpected move, they will make up a new fault in us, to recover. We are brainwashed and told a big story in a couple of seconds, and we are like in a dream with their lies. When they are uncovered, they set up an act, invent stories, names, dates and times; they involve other people and even believe their own stories. He will play the victim, the hurt, the one that suffers and the deceived one. He will make you believe that you are pressing, whipping and harassing him. He will make you think that you make it impossible for him to make a decision. He will make you think you only act on your own behalf.

Victims! Victims! Victims! They portray themselves as victims before their families, friends, colleagues and partners. They put on such a good act that other people pity them, forgive them their faults and cover up their misdeeds. In their conversations, in their past and present experiences, and in the things they share with us, they are always the victims. His attitudes, his arrogant expressions, his mood swings and the ups and downs of the relationship are attributed to the fact that he has been a victim.

According to him, he is the victim of former partners who did not appreciate him and did not value him as he deserved, so now he does not trust anyone. He claims to be the victim of bad experiences and disappointments that have made him "shut" his heart. It's the perfect excuse for not trusting us. Jerks use the fact of being "victims" to take advantage and give themselves an excuse to be such jerks. What else can you expect from someone who, every time you get close to him, has a shell around him and a whip in his mouth?

If your partner is a jerk, he will hardly make the small gesture of speaking to you with more consideration, more sweetness and tact, let alone will he stop considering himself a victim and take responsibility for his actions. With jerks we always have to forget our wounds and take things lightly. As if life was a circus! They go about getting into mischief and label it as nonsense; they do not admit their mistakes and do not even think of apologizing. You'd think that they were never taught manners. Jerks are masters at playing the victim, but it's up to you to fall or not into their vicious game.

If he cannot accept his mistakes

and apologize

he will not be able to make you happy.

If he plays always as victim

annihilate his psychological "game".

Characteristic # 14: **Relationship? At his convenience! Status? Never defined!**

Characteristic # 14: **Relationship? At his convenience! Status? Never defined!**

It turns out that, with jerks, we are rarely their partners, let alone taken seriously. Sometimes we are supposedly the love of their life. Most times, in fact, we are only their friends, "roommates," acquaintances or heaven knows what. Jerks show and tell others what they want depending on the occasion, the person and the environment where they are. If the jerk considers you not up to the place or the people he knows, or if he does not want to show that there is something between you and him, (without you noticing), he will introduce you by name only. He will use your name without your status with him, he will avoid physical contact with you (no caressing in front of his distinguished public) and he will treat you very politely and distantly. In this way, he will make others think you are his friend, another guest, or a person he is related to only professionally. Just an acquaintance, nothing serious.

If he is in a place where you can serve him as a good business card, he will introduce you as his girlfriend and maybe take your hand occasionally—just for appearances, nothing emotional. Do not doubt that at some point, he will leave you waiting in a chair in the middle of the activity or his work as if you were an acquaintance or another customer, but, you're so loony to see these things and react in time. The indicators that something is wrong pass before your eyes and you ignore them. You endure unnecessarily.

The relationship with a jerk is never defined, or rather said, no such relationship exists for them; it is only in your mind. You have sex, live together under one roof, "split" the expenses and responsibilities, but to a jerk, that does not mean a relationship as a couple exists, nor does it imply respect. They do not even mention the subject of the status of the relationship, and if a related subject ever surfaces, they evade it. When you want to know if you are his girlfriend or not, even though you are having sex or living under the same roof, he takes the question as a measure of pressure. He immediately jumps to the conclusion that you want to get married. And it's obvious: We want to know in 'what' we are investing our time, our feelings and our bodies in. It is normal that we want to know on what basis we stand and where the relationship is heading.

Any fool can understand this, except the jerk you have at your side. He will begin to find excuses to distance you and keep you uninvolved in his life. You're his "girlfriend" for sex, to bear his criticism, to "share" expenses, to help with his children (if any), to clean his apartment, to help him when they suspend his water or electricity services or to hide his financial secrets, but nothing else. In front of other women or his club of jerks, on the subject of the status of the relationship or his feelings, you are a friend. In his opinion, you're a casual friend, which he has in standby until somebody else he likes better or who has better qualities than you (according to him), comes along.

In front of his jerk friends, you are nothing serious. To his children, you are an aunt or a friend who takes them out for a walk. When you discover he is cheating with another woman (he has text messages or pictures that show his cheating), it turns out that he still does not consider as serious, the relationship you have with him. He will argue that he has been with you for only "a few days," despite having lived under the same roof for several months and having had sex for a while.

Jerks never lose, or at least that's what they think. Your status with them is never safe or stable. They are paper boats, easy to move, because they never grow true love toward their partners and themselves. They are like the dealer in a casino who shuffles the cards masterfully. You will never know which card he will pull from up his sleeve. In all of his games he will manipulate his cards, so you lose.

Jerks will always move unexpected chips to their favor. Being with a jerk is like walking on quicksand. It is walking on uncertain ground. Jerks do not talk about your place in their life. If you try to clarify the subject, they label it as unnecessary, as they take your place for granted, even if you have never talked about it. Your status has been very clear in the mind of the jerk from the beginning. You are with the jerk, but the jerk is not with you. He does not love you and has no plans for you in his future; therefore, he does not have to define your status in his life.

If he controls your relationship

at his convenience,

he will control your feelings

the same way.

Characteristic # 15: **Marriage? No way!**

Characteristic # 15: **Marriage? No way!**

We've all dreamed of seeing ourselves dressed in white, walking down the aisle and publicly declaring our love for our partner. It is something we long for and plan with great effort. However, a jerk is not fond of believing in marriage. If there would be a case where the thought of marriage had, in fact, passed through some remote spot in his mind, then you're confused: you are not going out with a jerk, but with a Martian. Jerks do not get married by choice but because of pressure from the girl's family, perhaps because she is pregnant, or for economic interest. Marriage is not what a jerk looks for. If there is a word that has never been a part of the vocabulary of the jerks, it is "marriage", at least not with us. Maybe you are excited about the relationship and have told him about your plans of someday being part of his life forever; he then freaks out and is never ever the same again. Compromising relationships are not part of his agenda, let alone a monogamous life.

Marriage is seen by jerks as the end of their outings and love adventures. Believe it or not, there have been jerks who have been married with much fanfare, even by the church, with both families and friends present. But his jerk mentality does not become part of his past. He will pretend for the first few months that everything is going wonderfully, trying to deceive those around him. What a hoax! The more calm and confident you are, the more the jerk will cheat on you, going out late with his buddies and saying with great conviction that he is working. Jerks do not help at home, and if they have children they would prefer that you take care of them or take them to day care, and that's the way he 'solves' the problem.

Jerks that have made the mistake of marrying have not exactly been saints, and most have ended their relationship in divorce. The few marriages with jerks that have survived, have done so because the jerk's wife has diminished, been subdued and "melted" like metal under fire at the whims of the jerk. The amazing thing is that when they get divorced, they shamelessly claim that their wife wanted to match wills with them, that she was nagging and demanded too much time, among thousands other excuses.

Jerks do not dare to stand firm and accept that they were not ready for marriage and that they did not give their best. They claim to be excellent husbands, that gave their partners a house and a few luxuries, however they never gave quality time, love, fidelity, or respect, much less knew how to bear with the responsibility of marriage.

If the jerk beside you is divorced, you will not be able to even talk to him about marriage. They live in the past; blaming you with faults that are not yours. They distrust and compare you and assume that a marriage by your side will be as absurd and doomed to fail as his former one. They think that marriage will initially be wonderful and then it will be a nightmare from which there will not be a way out. This way of thinking is just the reflection of his lack of interest and refusal to give up his life as a jerk. The belief that marriage does not work is imbued in the minds of the jerks. They do not want to accept that they are failures and that the only absurd thing is their behavior. However, they do nothing to stop being liers, dishonest, disloyal, unfaithful, 'show-offies', broken, self-centered, and sarcastic jerks.

Jerks hide behind lies since they do not think about changing their jerk mentality. They are unwilling to leave their binge drinking, women and friends. Jerks know how irresponsible it is on their behalf to play with our feelings and how useless they are at truly loving. For this only and true reason, they do not believe in marriage.

The man who loves you

would not want to leave any doubt

that you are his partner.

The man who loves you

would like to spend the rest of his days with you

and give you the best of his being.

His goal will be to take you to the altar

not for any reason

but for true love.

Characteristic # 16: **Children? Don't even dream about it!**

Characteristic # 16: **Children? Don't even dream about it!**

The arrival of a baby is a very special blessing. A baby is a motive for celebration and unsurpassable joy. A baby is even more special when it is conceived with the person you love. It is the act of giving life to a being that is part of both of you, a most sublime union. However, to the jerks, a baby is considered another headache. For them, a child is a symbol of more work and obligations, the cohesion of their freedom into a straitjacket.

If your jerk has children from some past relationship, they only represent for him an alimony increase and a weekend or two less, per month, to enjoy at large. As you go dreaming and yearning for this very special thing, his very own life inside you, the jerk sees the event as an outright disgrace. A child is a true disaster in his life. Jerks do not envision the arrival of a child, with you, as a blessing but as a calamity.

Most, if not all of the times that jerks have become parents, or rather "sperm banks," it has been because of a blunder: An unplanned event, that was the result of a hasty relationship based on the sex drive. The children are the product of relationships where the jerks' partners have been very emotionally involved, and the jerks also, but in their own carnal satisfaction; in situations where they have not measured the consequences of their lust. Some even dare to suggest abortion, but because of "remorse" from their parents' religious beliefs or because their partners did not agree to their proposal, they have become parents by force.

Jerks do not plan to have children, or at least not as quickly as us. For them, it would be better for children not to arrive! Once they have them, they avoid bearing the responsibility of raising and educating them. The most delicate and important steps are delegated to their partners, the child's grandparents or a day care center. They become parents by obligation and against their will. They are parents that are not involved with their children, in their activities and feelings. Parents who do not get to know their offspring because they are too busy to take some time off and get to know them. Parents that have not been involved in all stages of their children's lives or, better said, in almost none.

There are jerks who will say: "During the pregnancy of Jane Doe, I never got apart from her," or, "When Jane Doe was pregnant I was always there, I spoke to her belly and even played music to it." Of course! A baby in the belly is not a burden for a jerk. In the belly the baby still does not cry, does not ask for a diaper change, you don't need to feed or bathe him, nor is he an impediment to hanging out with his club of jerks. However, when babies are born, jerks rarely change a diaper or get up to look after them at night. Jerks only appear if it suits them to see their children for a weekend, a week or maybe once every six months, if not once a year. Jerks always promise to be model parents. They say their priority will be their children and they will be excellent providers, but at the moment of truth they abandon their responsibility, giving only crumbs to their children. Jerks are not fathers, because they never fully comply with their duty. The jerk, who on one hand spends a good salary and helps with extra expenses, on the other hand lacks time and affection for his children. The jerk who does not meet his financial responsibility tries to win the love of his children with "stories". They are one-hundred-percent jerks who have been parents only by chance and not by choice. Jerks are not loyal to our feelings. They are not devoted to a marriage without cheating, much less being parents who are involved with their children. They prefer to create the appearance of good parenting before others, rather than be the real thing. Best of all is that their children, as they grow up, discover for themselves the kind of jerk that their so-called father is.

Do not waste time trying to have a child with someone who does not deserve it. The attitude of your jerk clearly shows you that parenting is not in his interest and it's a responsibility he cannot assume, not because he needs more time, but because this role is too big for him.

The man who loves you
will want to have children with you.
His children will not be a burden
or a regret, and he will take
his parental responsibility very seriously.

Characteristic # 17: **"Meeting"** the family

Characteristic # 17: **"Meeting" the family**

Meeting your partner's family has never been an easy process; you feel insecure and fear to be rejected. There is a mixture of feelings that you fight by trying to please his family and gain acceptance. You want to engage in a sincere friendship with his mother, because she is a woman like you and usually knows her offspring better than you do. You are interested in getting close to them, to know how they think and what they like. You want to let them know how much you love their son and to show them your affection. You want to make them a second family and even want to feel like them. You expect to establish a dialogue about their situations and concerns and get close to them all the way, because his family is part of him. This cluster of desires and anxieties creates a very intense tension and makes this first visit to meet his family, an extremely stressful visit.

You look forward to the day when you finally get to meet his family. You are moved by the genuine desire to strengthen the ties that bind you to him.

But do not worry about this, because getting to know his family does not happen so quickly with a jerk. You may already have gone out several times; perhaps he already knows your whole family. He even knows your dog or your cat, however you don't even know his sister's name, and surely he hasn't told you where his family lives.

When you finally get to meet them and find out they are great, the jerk stops you from spending time with them, probably because he fears that an indiscreet relative will tell you small details that you shouldn't know, at least for now. You will notice that visits to the home of his family will not be as frequent and long as you wanted. This does not mean he will stop visiting his family, but he will visit more often without you, even if you live with him.

Jerks are afraid that you will charm his relatives, and that they will start defending you more than him. They fear not being able to commit their 'crimes' freely, because they will be censored by their families. A jerk knows he is a disloyal person, so he prefers that you don't get too close to his relatives. He will not want to balance the scale against himself. When a jerk finds out that you have built a friendship with his mother to the point where you tell her how he sometimes treats you, he will feel that you are undermining the credibility that he has with his mother. He will make up comments and situations to cast a doubt on the words and actions of his mother, so you will stop seeing her as your ally. He will say things like, "I do not like you telling everything to my parents," "I do not like loading them with problems," "I do not want you 'filling' my mom's head"; "My mother and I don't have a very good communication. She is always pushing me, and if you tell her things about me, you will make her push me even more."

Jerks do not want their families on your side, supporting you. He will always like to be the gentle little lamb in front of his parents. He will try to be the poor helpless victim who has had no luck with women. Of course, your bond with his family is a threat to his behavior as a jerk and his disguise as a victim.

The man who loves you and wants
to spend the rest of his life with you,
will not be afraid of you meeting his family
nor that they could love you.

Characteristic # 18: **"Get involved with my kids . . . but not too much!"**

Characteristic # 18: **"Get involved with my kids . . . but not too much!"**

It turns out that if your jerk has kids, it is obvious that you would like to meet them, please them, and be nice to them, because they will become yours, even if they live far away. You will want to be part of their lives and make them part of yours. You will want to know what they like and dislike about you. You'll want to know if they feel comfortable with you and if they are sad or happy by your side. In short, you want to know everything about them, because now they are part of your life.

It turns out that your jerk, at first, looks at this issue in a very proper and most logical way. As you spend time with his children trying to know them, you start suggesting ideas about how he could improve his relationship with them, and this 'idea' no longer pleases him. This unsolicited intervention in the upbringing and education of his children upsets him. It turns out that, since his responsibility as a father is far from being even satisfactory, sometimes his children feel more comfortable with you than with him. So, in front of his children the jerk treats you like a friend; he will introduce you as his "buddy" or call you by a nickname. Your jerk has not bothered to formally introduce you, nor has he spoken clearly about your position in his life. We could say he even seems to be cautious at this point. Remember, your jerk does not want anything formal with you, you are his "solved for now," so there is no point for his kids seeing you as his girl. It doesn't matter if his closet is full of your clothes and his kids know that you sleep in his bed, you're still something like a nanny. How ironic, right?

Their children suffer because despite the refusal of the jerk, you continue to enter into their hearts. They are hungry for affection rather than possessions. They feel inhibited from freely and openly expressing their love to you because the jerk limits them. They suffer when they feel that you will not last in their lives, thanks to your jerk being a coward. Even though jerks are not the best in their roles as fathers, they claim they do not want to see their children suffering from involving them with a new partner if things do not work out. However the place where things do not work, is inside his head. They start to go out with you, carrying preconceived ideas and tangled fears, still living in their dark past. They make hasty conclusions about you and about the idea of a future with you, while you give yourself whole-heartedly, and are busy giving his kids the affection and love that they deserve and so badly need.

Their children do not get involved with you as they would want to, because they do not see a sincere commitment from your jerk to you. Jerks are extremely stupid; when they have a partner that could not care less to integrate with their children, and does not care to identify with them, love them, please them and treat them as if they were her own, then the jerks crawl, cry and humiliate themselves and feel that they will die for those partners. On the other hand, when they have a partner who loves them and loves their children, treats them well and wants the best for them, they don't value her. They sabotage the love that grows in their kids with comments, often made as jokes, with the objective that they too will begin to see flaws in you, to keep them from loving you.

When you're with his kids all day, you take them out to have fun, for lunch or to the movies, or you buy them things they wish for and spend time treating them as your children, the jerk will start to feel displeasure with this. He fears that you will fill the void he has caused on his children, when he is with them. Now that you feel that you are starting to be a family, the jerk no longer values your efforts.

When you decide to call him because it's been three hours since he left his job and he has not even called to see how you and his children are, he answers with disgust and even defiantly argues that you want to control him. He yells at you, hangs up the phone and turns violent. Without a doubt, one-hundred-percent jerk! In other words, he cannot understand in his narrow brain that you want to share with him the experiences you shared with his children that day and that his children and you are eager to see him. No, the stupid man only thinks of himself. He just thinks, "Do not control me, do not push me," and, "I don't have to give account for my actions." Every time he leaves you to care for his children for a long time without a valid reason, he invents a drama to divert the attention from where he was at and what he was doing. The reality is that he counted on having a babysitter to take care of his kids, went out and forgot his responsibility as a parent and partner.

If your jerk does not want to give you a son, because he sees it as a burden, an additional mouth to feed, or more work; if he is not properly involved with his children or yours, and if he does not know or care about assuming his parental responsibility (beyond alimony), thank God that he does not give you the privilege of being a mother, because he does not deserve being a father. Let a real man give you that wonderful privilege and enjoy it fully with you. A man of integrity is one who takes that important role with full responsibility, not a jerk who is a thousand light-years away from being a man and a good father.

The man who loves you will introduce you as his girlfriend to his kids and will encourage respect and love amongst you.

Characteristic # 19: **Memories or ghosts?**

Characteristic # 19: **Memories or ghosts?**

There is nothing more sad and painful than finding out that your partner lives in the past. The last jerk that came into my life had a huge problem with his memories. His memories of the past were not good, and although he even claimed to not want to have anything to do with his former partners and even criticized them to death, he often remembered them, especially on important dates such as Valentine's Day, Christmas Eve or Christmas Day. His eyes turned watery when he mentioned them. He would turn super-sensitive and nostalgic, remembering moments lived with his former partners, and he would tend to self-destruct.

On one occasion we went to a restaurant on Valentine's Day and the jerk suddenly said, "I can not believe it, at this same table and in that same chair you're sitting, Susie Q. sat on a day like today." Bastard! At that time I thought, "What the hell am I doing with this jerk? What an asshole!" It was then when I realized I was with the wrong person in the wrong place.

Sometimes you talk about how much you enjoy visiting certain places, eat certain foods, how much you like some pets or you talk about the perfume that you love, and your jerk says, "Jane Doe used to like that also," or "Have you tried the steak with this spices? Jane Doe loved them," or, "Umm! This perfume reminds me of something . . . Ms. *So-and-So* used it all the time."

When sharing with your jerk, you note that his memories became ghosts. Ghosts that chase you, rob your strength and make you feel depressed. And it gives you something to think about: Could this jerk still be in love with one of his previous girlfriends? Why is he so involved still, after she hurt him so badly? You have no other choice than to think: has he made up his partner's fault, and was he the cause of everything? Is he being reproachful of himself now?

The answer is that your jerk is not in love with his former girlfriends, and he doesn't care for them either. What happens is that his remorse for the times that he did not correspond to their love and sacrifice is killing him. He is being killed by his own conscience (if he has any), knowing he did not act with loyalty, respect, sincerity and commitment. His previous partners, the same as you, were devoted to loving him and making him happy, respecting and valuing him in a way he did not deserve.

He is tormented remembering that his jerk behavior opened a Pandora's Box, harmful to those who loved him and even to himself. He hurt others by not measuring his actions; he destroyed what both of them had built, or rather, what his partners built. Blaming his former partners, he intends to clear his own faults.

Jerks' memories, like ghosts, get out of their graves when you least expect it, come to the door of your relationship and sabotage it. These ghosts keep the soul of the jerk lost; a sorrow they deserve for not having valued what they had, but a sorrow we do not have and we do not deserve to suffer ourselves. These ghosts do not allow him to accept and let go of the past, because he lives by trying to disguise what happened, dragging along feelings of guilt, anger and frustration. They do not heal, and what is worse, they cannot overcome their mistakes, because they keep pretending they are the victims to elude their faults. These ghosts that he creates are obstacles that do not let him create a new mature and stable relationship.

Jerks need to drag these 'ghosts' around to appear as hurt, suffering and misunderstood. Jerks want to live with their ghosts, to have something to fall back on and to say they did the right thing at some point. They keep the ghosts close to have an excuse for acting even more "jerkish" with us. They love to live from memories, in order to defend themselves for being what they are. They keep photos, letters, cards and gifts from the past instead of cultivating a positive relationship in the present. They rush to start new relationships without giving themselves some time. They are afraid of being seen alone and losing their title of great conqueror. They did not live the past fully, they don't live the present and will not live the future, because they do not change their lifestyle. They live with the idea of what could have been, when they know they didn't do what was required to maintain a quality relationship. They do not do it in their current relationship because they don't have the courage to be men. They are mediocre, and they are jerks.

He who lives in the past can't love you.

He who uses you to forget, doesn't love you.

Characteristic # 20: **The ultra religious!**

Characteristic # 20: **The ultra religious!**

There are two extremes with jerks on the subject of religion. There are very devoted jerks that spend time inside the church, occupying important positions in their denominations and even knowing the Bible from beginning to end. They preach to the congregation or actively participate in the catechisms. They cry at Mass on Sundays, and they even recite long and dramatic prayers, to be considered most devout. Surprisingly, these are the same jerks that, upon leaving the church and getting home, treat you like shit, hide a lover, consider you of little value and don't give a damn about your feelings. Where did the devout Christian go? His attitude is demeaning and degrading, totally opposite to what he shows in church. They fall deeply into what is often criticized in the Bible: lying, cheating and adultery. They have two lives: one is the life of appearance and holiness, and the other a life of paganism and carnal lust. They are driven by their low passions, of course, except when seen by those to whom they want to look like a gentleman.

The other type of religious jerk is the one who never visits the church, does not like to talk about religious subjects or read religious literature, but in times of trouble, turns to the false disguise of sanctifying himself with religion. This jerk sometimes gives the appearance of even being an atheist, shows no interest in being a practitioner of any religion and sometimes even makes fun of devout Christians. For him, religion is a mechanism of manipulation and control. This is the same jerk who asks for a "chance" upon being discovered in adultery because: "God in His Word does not judge the sinner but forgives him." It's the same jerk who asks you to give him a chance when you leave him and recites almost by heart that "everything in the relationship will be different, because God has brought us together . . ." What these two types of jerks have in common is that they use religion as they please. When religion hits them with the truth of their adultery, their lies, their deceit and all of their vileness, they hide behind the fact that the love of God makes them new creatures and forgives them their sins. They brainwash us with their word games to make us believe that they have changed and are "new creatures". They want to lead us into believing that, if we believe in God and we love them, we must do as Jesus did: pardon all his sins and cast them into the sea (and into oblivion!). They want to make us see that their sins, "though they are red as crimson, they shall be like wool" (Isaiah 1:18). They hope to be accepted back as if nothing happened. No matter how many times the jerk promises to change without honoring his words, we have to forgive him without bringing back the past. We must forgive as Jesus did, seventy times seven, the same sin (as if we were God!.) But guess what? We are not Jesus Christ; we are made of flesh and bone. We can not allow ourselves to be run over and be used by someone hiding behind God's love and forgiveness.

The Bible is very clear when it condemns adultery, deceptive eyes, a lying tongue and feet that are swift to do evil. God hates scheming minds and licentious lips. God is proud of the righteous, who do not sell their conscience, and who call sin by its name (something jerks cannot do). God is proud of the men whose yes is yes, and his no is no, and represent Him with dignity.

Many interpret the Bible as they please, believe in secular ideas and try to hide behind passages of the Bible taken out of context. But the Word of God is unmovable and doesn't change. Do not let yourself fall into the jerk's traps. Each time he uses passages of the Bible to dominate and manipulate your mind, remind him or quote the full text. With these words I am not saying you should get deep into religion or to learn the Bible from beginning to end, but I urge you to get to know about God and confront the lies of your jerk. Seek God's direction and expose that impostor you have by your side. Pray, even if it's just in your mind: "God, help me to have understanding and do not allow me to be persuaded by an evil mind. Give me courage to get out from this unhealthy relationship." God, better than anyone, knows your jerk, his intentions, his movements, delusions and the plans he is plotting against you. God, in his infinite wisdom, also knows about your anguish better than anyone else. Commit your ways to God and He will guide you at all times.

If your jerk, after being exposed, suddenly becomes ultra religious and takes refuge under the cloak of religion or God's forgiveness, it means he is exhausting his last resorts, because he knows the battle is lost, and you're close to not falling into his trap anymore!

Our bad decisions are the result of not consulting God first.

Characteristic # 21: **Understanding, submissive and all that they need**

Characteristic # 21: **Understanding, submissive and all that they need**

A badly unbalanced scale! The relationship with a jerk is like a lopsided scale. One "side" is obviously giving more than it is receiving, and that side is you. All on his side is transient and ephemeral. While the jerk decides whether you can or can't be the one to spend with him one month more or just one day, he will expect you to be an understanding woman at all times. The jerk wants you submissive and devoted in every situation, even when he yells and humiliates you. You almost get dragged by the hair or killed with a "wooden knife," and yet he expects you to be nice to him in everything. You will not be able to demand, complain, voice your opinion or anything like that. You have to be everything the jerk needs. Right! And on the other side of the scale? Crumbs! Jerks only give the crumbs of what they have. Time?, only when they have some left; that is, if they do not have anything more fun to do. They listen when it suits them; they pay attention and are affectionate only when they want sex, and that is if there is no one in "the street" to give them "something." They try to manipulate us as if we were their rag dolls.

One would think we are in a classroom and they are the teachers. They shut us up, they limit us, they "teach" us, grade us and assess how good or bad we are. They take away our favorite fun activities, and we go to recess only if we have been good girls, at their discretion. They use us as they please, and we are tied to their will without escape. And you know? There is something that I am sure of: there are better "candidates" out there.

Remember that to be with a jerk you have to constantly sacrifice. You sacrifice your time and miss work, studies or social activities to be with him. However, do not forget that on his days off he has other plans, which do not include you. He prefers to be with his friends and fill his house with people, to be with everyone except you. You go to incredible lengths to accommodate him, an effort that you do not make even for yourself. You do thousands of things to spend more time by his side, and he does not seem to notice. You prepare the house, the right atmosphere, candles, tablecloth, the perfect dinner and put forth all your effort and love, but still the jerk is not happy. With him, everything is a cause for complaint! He always looks discouraged and wears a sad face. As if he is fed up with everything!

Could it be that so much sweetness overwhelms him? No! It is that the scumbag does not know how to appreciate it.

I remember like yesterday that when I was in a relationship with a one-hundred-percent-to-the-fourth-power jerk, I left my business several times just to surprise him. I stopped monitoring my employees and made a huge list of things-to-do just to please him. I got up very early and went to the mall first thing in the morning. I bought candles, oils, two bouquets of white roses, two glass vases, a CD with instrumental music, new bed sheets, chocolate strawberries and Godiva white chocolate. I spent more than half a day shopping. Then I went to his apartment and did an extensive cleanup, which took me well into the afternoon. I decorated the room with the two glass vases, placed a bouquet of white roses in each one, then placed candles around the room, put on the new bed sheets, lit incense, turned on the air conditioner in the room so the smell would spread around and as a finishing touch, I scattered white rose petals across the floor and bed. I showered, got dressed and anxiously waited for him. When he arrived he was a little surprised, but not as I expected. I asked him to bathe, and started the instrumental CD I had bought as he entered the bedroom. I asked him to lie face down, massaged his body while feeding him chocolate-covered strawberries and Godiva white chocolate. I massaged him all over, leaving him so relaxed he fell asleep and started snoring. And how did he pay me back? Weeks later I found a text message on his mobile phone saying, "My dear, thank you for the candles and oil, I love you very much, *Yary*." The jerk took my idea and used it to win the heart of another. Another jerk had the nerve to hold conversations with his former girlfriend behind my back and even invited her to stay in our house without my knowledge, saying it was because she had problems with her new partner. What a jerk! He definitely won the world title!

I went through many bad experiences with these two jerks. It turns out that one of these jerks has three children whom I still love, since it was not their fault to have a jerk for a father. I always wanted their children to feel comfortable, and above all, loved with me. I noticed that their rooms were not decorated, and that they did not feel a connection to their rooms when it was their turn to spend the weekend with him. For this reason, I suggested some changes to their rooms. One of the changes I suggested was removing the factory-installed protective plastic covering on the mattresses, because they were too hot and noisy at night. I also suggested painting the walls and putting up some decorations. I talked about installing curtains to keep out some light, so the children could rest a bit more in the morning, because they complained that the sunlight bothered them in the early hours. I suggested installing air conditioners in their rooms, as they slept with fans and only he had air conditioning. After obtaining his approval, I met with his children and asked them about the theme and color of their rooms' decorations. As soon as I had all the details, I went shopping. With my money, I bought pink paint for the girls' room and blue paint for the boy's room, as they requested. I bought butterflies, brushes, rollers, trays, decorative materials, glitter and glue. I again asked one of my employees to take care of my business, and I started to paint two of the girls' bedroom walls according to their wishes. While the paint dried, I decorated the wings of the butterflies with glitter and sequins. I was really exhausted, but at the same time I was excited because I thought of the excitement in the girls' faces when they would see their room.

He came at night, and upon seeing the room his first words were, "I do not like that color! Why would you use such a bright color? And besides, it is semi-gloss—that is so outdated!" I felt like a slap in the face, and again I realized I was in the wrong place with the wrong person. I wasn't expecting a fanfare for painting his daughters' room, but at least expected his gratitude. I was wondering why, if I had invited him to go with me to buy the paint, and he refused, and then asked me to take care of this project, was he criticizing me now?"

Do you want to know what happened in the end? I told him that if he didn't like the color, he should paint it, and that I would not decorate his son's room. Paradoxically, both his daughters loved the color and the butterflies when they saw them. But I had made my decision. I did not decorate any more, and all the projects that were pending in the apartment were never completed. I had lost the desire to finish the rooms because of that bad experience. They stayed half-finished. The kids were disappointed as well, and the jerk never apologized. The lesson I learned from this was that, no matter what I could have given or sacrificed, for the jerk, it would never be enough.

If it is you

the one that always must go the extra mile

so both of you can dwell in harmony,

then it is you who is supporting

something that was over a long time ago

or that maybe never existed.

Characteristic # 22: **I do not care about your suffering**

Characteristic # 22: **I do not care about your suffering**

Jerks make us feel confident at first, so we naively tell them about our saddest experiences. In doing so, we wrongly expect understanding and protection from them, but no . . . jerks use our pain to open our old wounds and make them worse. We cry many tears while entrusting our secrets, but that does not make them more sensitive. The jerks ask, "What hurt you most in your past relationship?" "Which things you didn't like your partner to do to you?" "Which things would make you drive off from your partner?" "What would make you end a relationship?"

When we are asked these questions, we confess as if we were before a priest. We are unsuspecting and give them all the details, thinking they are listening carefully to avoid making the same mistakes with us, but we are wrong. They are recording everything in great detail with the goal of making us suffer even more. They repeat exactly the same actions that greatly harmed us in the past. Worse yet, they make them more serious and bigger, deepening our wounds. They record our suffering in their minds, not to relieve it, but to destroy us, to defend themselves when their "jerkish" actions are uncovered.

Recording in their minds what other jerks did to us makes them feel they have "something" they can use as an excuse. They seem to tell themselves, "If he did that to her, I can do it too, and do even worse." Remember that for jerks, being at the top of everything makes them feel better. This way they feel they have the authority to hurt us again mercilessly. This way, they have the perfect excuse for their dirty tricks, and can then say to themselves, "She's not suffering too much, because she has been through this before." "Her former partner did worse." "She is not acting this way because of what I am doing, but because she is very sensitive for everything that she has gone through, and now I'm paying for it." Our past pain makes them feel with the right and the confidence to hurt us again without remorse.

For jerks, our past holds not even a thousandth part of the pain they have suffered. Jerks always feel they have suffered more than the rest of the world, and especially, more than us. They pity themselves in their pain (which has been caused by them) and become greater jerks each day. If we are suffering in a relationship with them, this fact will be omitted, just because "we are being too sensitive." Our suffering, pain and frustrations are cast aside and viewed as irrelevant, superfluous and as a control mechanism for them. Flee from the insensitive; if he makes you cry and does not mind your pain, he is a jerk of the worst kind.

He who does not care about your suffering,

neither will consider

how deeply he will hurt you.

Characteristic # 23: **The blessed distrust!**

Characteristic # 23: **The blessed distrust!**

Romantic relationships are like a boomerang; they work based on reactions. You both begin the relationship with enthusiasm, because it is a new beginning. It is a new opportunity, a change. Emotions and physical changes that were believed to be lost, are felt. Suddenly you feel alive again; renewed.

Everything is perfect until your jerk starts messing up your life. He starts being indiscreet and compares, criticizes, and judges you. He does not mince his words; he offends you and hangs the phone up on you. He no longer finds you that attractive, he starts isolating from you and seems indifferent. He evades intimate moments and no longer has sex with the same frequency or desire as before. Given this unloving and even distant attitude, it is natural that distrust toward the jerk grows inside you. You start doubting that he is the perfect partner for you. You even doubt that he can fill you with the love and attention you need. You start feeling jealous and suspecting that something is amiss in your relationship.

While you are dating a jerk you are faced with many situations that give you a feeling that something is not right. Maybe at first you do not know what it is exactly, but you know there's something that is not doing any good to your mind and your body. Perhaps some time has already gone by, and you have been unable to identify what makes you feel weird, uncomfortable, anxious, and as if you were floating without any direction.

Jerks are excellent actors as well as excellent manipulators. With them, we are in a constant chess game in which we see love in the opening, we get distracted, and by doing so, we miss several of his moves. Jerks make their moves quickly and skillfully without us noticing. They vilely and blatantly lie before our eyes. They lie with their relaxed and unruffled faces, as if nothing was happening. They lie all the time, in a natural and almost imperceptible way. The get so involved in their lies that they even come to consider them as the absolute truth. If they are caught in a lie or deception, they make up another lie, another and another, all of them with a well planned and premeditated setup. When all this swarm of lies is exposed with explicit evidence, they start manipulating the facts. They use phrases said months before, gestures, arguments or mere pretexts from the past to conceal their deceptive nature. They distort their moves to try to show that we are to blame. They manipulate all of their mess to prove their "innocence."

If your partner uses
manipulation and acting
to control your mind,
it is clear that he does not respect you
and underestimates your value.
The man who loves you
will not manipulate you.
You will not have to distrust him
because with his love
he will show you the truth.

Characteristic # 24: **When they retreat**

Characteristic # 24: **When they retreat**

Here is when the relationship reaches a point where you know too many things about him. You know about his "masks" and his defects, and it is here that he chooses to retreat. When you demand attention, quality time and honesty above all, he acts normal, but he is horrified. When you question his moves and want to be part of his life or keep track of what he does with his time (when he vanishes), you have reached the "tipping point", and he retreats. When you wish to know what he devotes his time to when he is not with you, it's already too much for him; he feels cornered. When you want more unity amongst yourselves and not something superfluous, be prepared: You will get stabbed. Your jerk starts to feel self-conscious about getting into mischief freely. He is bothered with tolerating your "stupidity" and claims that you want to control him, that he has no freedom anymore. He insists on labeling you as possessive, arguing that your lifestyles are very different and that he can not bear the situation anymore. Does this sound familiar? This is when you begin to set your limits and claim your rights, because you want to live the rest of your life by his side and thus, fit. When you finally understand that you have the right to ask, demand and complain, your jerk starts to retreat.

Jerks do not want to sign a final covenant, firm and sincere. Jerks prefer to live freely, doing at large everything they please. They do not want anyone "laying the cards on the table" and ending their game. It is not in their plans to give in, let go of their friends, the outdoors, the drinks, the parties and the women that are non-demanding easy catches . . . Plainly and simply, they decide they can not be at your side because you want a clear and transparent relationship based on equality, honesty and mutual respect. In other words, they are not ready for a relationship and need to flee.

The man who really loves you,
will not want to be apart from you
much less flee when he feels loved.

Characteristic # 25: **They cause separation and boredom**

Characteristic # 25: **They cause separation and boredom**

When the relationship has become a little more formal, your jerk feels uncomfortable, cornered, harassed and shy about doing what he pleases. He makes up the excuse that you want to formalize the relationship and that you are "going too fast." He argues that he is getting involved and is not ready for a relationship, and seeks endless silly excuses to push you away. He recognizes that he cannot bear the responsibility of making you happy, giving you respect and emotional stability. However, he neither has the guts to face you and tell you that he is not a man but a jerk and that he wants to walk like a stray dog, living for adventures and wild passions. The easiest thing for the jerk is to create cracks and divisions in the relationship. How? Very easy. He will work hard to damage all that you have wanted to build for you both. He will leave you alone more time than necessary, he will not mince his words and will spend more time with his friends and hobbies. He will show indifference, dispassion and insensitivity. He will neglect you and criticize you even more.

By making you feel less important or of no importance in his life, he will try to make you weary. He aims to bring you loneliness and emptiness, triggering the need for someone to fill the emotional and sexual void he has created in you. Your jerk is only trying to get you into a vicious circle. He tries to transform your feelings of love for him into despair, emptiness and pain. He wishes you to begin asking yourself if you really want to stay in this relationship with him. Maybe you wonder, "Why, if he doesn't want to be with me, he doesn't honestly tell me?" The truth is that your jerk will never tell you: He does not have the nerve or the guts to honestly talk with you, because he is not a man . . . he is a jerk.

He does not have the courage to look at you in the face and say, "I'm falling in love with you and I admit that we are entering a more formal stage in our relationship, which scares me because it requires a change in my lifestyle, and I do not want to feel controlled". He does not have the guts to tell you, "This relationship is taking an unexpected turn for me, I think we are rushing; there is too much formality or commitment and I don't want it, because I don't feel I'm ready to love this way." He could even be more honest and say, "I do not want to stay with you, I have evaluated my feelings and I feel that I don't love you the same way you love me, so we should split. I do not want to deceive you or hurt you."

Never expect this kind of confession from a jerk. Jerks are cowards when facing their decisions. They do not want to tell you the truth, not because he cares for you and is afraid to hurt you, but because he knows that you, when feeling hurt and unrequited, would bring forth the truth about his life before the eyes of others. He knows you are going to expose him. Deep inside, what your jerk is worried about is that, if you leave carrying with you all those negative feelings toward him, he will be exposed in front of everyone. Upon your exposing him, he will not be able to fool others and will lose his macho image. It will not be easy for him to get laid with someone else using the lies he made you believe in. Therefore it is easier for your jerk to bring you down, push you away and cause fractures and wounds in you, so you get tired and leave. By inflicting these wounds he will cause you to do something stupid to get you out of his life. In this way he will find the perfect excuse to tell others that the relationship did not work because of you.

He wants you to get tired and to make you leave by creating confusion and frustration inside you. This way he will avoid your immediate anger and will cause you to feel very guilty. Meanwhile, you, not really knowing what took him away from you, will be left susceptible and desolate. You will seek ways of knowing what led him to this decision. This desire to recover him will make you a "sitting duck" for him to use again. Each time the jerk calls, looks at you or sends an email, you will think that he wants to make up, and you will be a "sitting duck". The only thing that you will accomplish upon falling at his feet will be to end up in his bed, being used again. Just what the jerk wants: to use you without having to feel anything for you. He only looks for someone to be there for a night of passion, without having to involve his feelings.

The jerk will prefer that you make the decision about a break up, confirming his strategy of being the victim and the one that suffers. Again, he will make the move of asking for more time and claiming being confused, and he will take refuge in indifference, and fears that will cause you to feel bored. He will make up all sorts of excuses and pretexts to get you to end up cornered with no other choice than to leave.

If he cannot be honest enough

to show you his feelings,

he is not a trustworthy man

and does not deserve you.

If he is looking to cause

a separation between you,

it is because he is not convinced

of wanting to stay by your side

and yet more important, he does not love you.

Characteristic # 26: **Suddenly, "I have a lot of work to do!"**

Characteristic # 26: **Suddenly, "I have a lot of work to do!"**

As jerks are cowards, they try multiple reasons to end the relationship. They project their frustrations and fears onto you. They make up all sorts of complaints, problems and disagreements. As they say, they are "nitpickers". All these flaws, situations, disagreements and displeasures (most of which are of no importance) are in pursuit of only one purpose: to destroy all hopes and commitment to your relationship. They do not want to let the relationship become an intimate and profound one. He will say that you no longer dress up, that you have changed, that you want to control him, that he can not bear your family, that his friends told him this or that, among many other things, to get you away from his life. If, after he makes up all of this, you still have not gone away because you love him, he will use his best trick last, suddenly saying: "I have a lot of work to do," or, translated, "I have no time for you. "Jerks really know the best way to get what they want, because, who is going to go and complain to his boss? Faced with this trick, you're "between a rock and a hard place", because you have to accept it. I think any woman would get tired of a relationship in which she could hardly see her partner, where she is in second place, or rather last, because his daily schedule is too full to see her. Now is when the jerk begins to notice how effective his plan and his efforts are, and you begin to feel more alone than ever. He even enjoys noticing that his plan is going along just perfect.

With the excuse of his job, he will go out in a hurry in the morning without saying a word or even saying goodbye. Continuing with this trite excuse (he can use many others), he will not have time during the day to give you a call or send you a message. His work will be the excuse for leaving his office late and not answering your calls when you want to know where he is. Because of his job, he will not take days off to dedicate them to you, and he will be tired all the time, but not enough to turn off his phone and stop answering calls from everyone else (except from you). You will be last on his "busy" schedule, thus fulfilling his greater purpose: letting you know by his actions that he neither wants you to be part of his life nor meddle in his affairs.

Exhausted, we are flooded with loneliness, emptiness and confusion. We fervently hope to find someone to be with us, to make us remember that we still feel and are worth a lot. We start to feel overwhelmed; we go through thousands of thoughts, even of infidelity. We are pushed against the wall and forced to use an escape that he takes advantage of to make us the ones to blame.

Love he who gives you the first
place in his daily schedule.

Characteristic # 27: **The perfect excuse . . .
The damned Mars and Venus caves!**

Characteristic # 27: **The perfect excuse . . . The damned Mars and Venus caves!**

Since you do not understand the attitude of your jerk, you despair. You think he has another woman (which it still is true!). You think you are no longer attractive, you are filled with complexes and frustration, you think love is over, you even think that you are unable to keep a partner. In these desperate times you start reading self-help books and books for couples, looking for what you have been doing wrong. You even decide to go with him to the church he attends (which perhaps is not the one you like the most!). You come up with all sorts of strategies to make the relationship work. You try thousands of ways; you quote magazines, documentaries or news stories to entice him to put some effort into the relationship.

Suddenly, you come up with the idea of recommending or citing the book *Men are from Mars, Women are from Venus*. With this book, you try to encourage him and make him talk about what is happening to him. You try to do something to avoid this estrangement between you two. Maybe you bought the book, maybe he bought it after you recommended it so much. Perhaps he borrowed it or only heard what you said a few times about the "cave dialogue". The cave, according to the book, is where "men" hide (like Neanderthals), for fear of a face-to-face dialogue, because they are cowards. Although the book clearly explains the metaphor and really intends it to be a helpful tool, your jerk will twist it to his convenience. The book says that if you give him full confidence and the space he needs, at some point he will come out of his cave and tell you what is happening to him. Sure! But the jerk in your life twists everything around to use as he pleases. As a jerk, he ends up throwing away the good part and taking only what suits him.

You begin to realize that the damn cave and all the time in the world are nothing but tales molded to his convenience. You regret a thousand times having told him about the cave, because now, he takes the book out and quotes it so you leave him alone. Jerks hide behind this fallacy so you do not question them when they turn their backs to us in bed without saying a single word. They use this as an excuse to end conversations that do not suit them, and they do not allow us to express freely.

When a man loves you
the last thing he will do is pull you apart and
hide in cheap ideologies
to get you out of his life.
He will seek to talk with you
in order to reach an understanding
and clarify any doubts.

Characteristic # 28: **In his cave or in his own world?**

Characteristic # 28: **In his cave or in his own world?**

Everything in life has two sides to it. The cave theory for men is designed as a tool for self-help and to encourage their partners to understand them. But for jerks it has no other meaning than the perfect excuse to lock themselves in their own world. Jerks hide in their own world with intent and premeditation. Their world, that is, their friends, their "hanging out," parties, alcohol, their other women, their concerns and everything they make up are only excuses to keep us out. If your partner really loved you, he would notice that you are trying by all means to reach his heart in different ways. He would try to look for the most effective and least hurtful way to let you know when he needs time and space and tell you why he does need it. The locking-in and long meditations isolating you from his life are not natural. If the isolation is hurtful, sudden and without reason, it means the feeling of love is not real. His doubts about the relationship with you make him clear a space for third parties and negative situations, causing disaster between the two of you.

This does not mean we are not supposed to have time to be alone . . . no. We all, at some point, need solitude to find ourselves, but it is not normal to do it frequently or for such a long time. The "spaces" created by your jerk are intended to reject you and get you out of his life.

When love is real and true,

you don't exclude your loved one, instead,

you make him part of your life.

Characteristic # 29: "**Don't put pressure on me, you want to control me!**"

Characteristic # 29: "**Don't put pressure on me, you want to control me!**"

Everyone at some point needs space to be alone. We do not have the same mood every day. There are days when we burst into tears and days when we laugh about everything. There are days when we would have preferred not to get out of bed, days when everything makes us feel bothered or shattered. This does not mean we are bipolar or that we have psychological problems. The human being is like the sea: It has high and low tides, and the wind moves it at will.

However, in the case of jerks we face a violent sea. A sea of turbulent and deceiving waters which is not only moved by the wind, but by everything around it no matter how small, will cause a storm. They confuse the term "space" with "isolation". An example of this is that every time you want to touch him, hug him or show him your feelings, he takes refuge in the famous phrase "I need my space." They use this phrase at will, depriving us of free speech and destroying our desire to be by their side. We are rejected, treated unemotionally and restricted from expressing our love freely, only because they need "space" or "time."

Ironically, with their attitude, jerks do not show that they need time. Instead, their way of speaking to us and their gestures show rejection. We are replaced by their favorite pastimes, their buddies, video games, parties or even by a nap. The space he asks for and demands serves not to comfort his soul, but to show that he does not want to stay involved with you or keep giving you more space so you can bond with him.

For jerks, having their space does not mean time for meditation and relaxation. Their claim for space is caused in many cases by remorse. Deep inside, they cannot feel at ease knowing that they are not honoring the integrity and the covenant of love and trust that we offer them by dedicating all our time and love. Their conscience reproaches them, but is silenced by vices, parties and more lies. Imagine! It must be overwhelming for them to think all day about the lies they have told and remember them in their entirety to avoid being caught in a contradiction somewhere.

Jerks are forced to recall faces, names, places and events they attended with other women to avoid mistakes. They need to remember every detail, not only just what position they used and with whom, but also where, to avoid mistakes when their partners remind them of an intimate moment they shared weeks or months ago. That is why jerks rarely use your name: to avoid mistakes. They replace your name with "gorgeous," "baby," and "sweetie," titles they confer on all alike. This feature is closely related to projection.

Jerks insist that you change, that you improve, that you don't do this, that you don't say that, that you please their friends and do many other things that they would not do or say themselves. Throughout the relationship you have to endure a lot of pressure; let yourself be controlled and changed at his will, in other words, you have to stop being yourself. However, he does not let you complain about his isolation, his deceptions, his abuse and infidelity. If you complain, the jerk will accuse you of putting pressure on him, being very insistent, and screwing his life up. Jerks intend for us to deal with their mood swings, indifference and unexplained isolation, and above all, they do not allow us to inquire about those matters.

Facing his sudden lack of love without asking for an explanation is totally unfair. You go after him, trying to get close, and it's like walking on eggshells: all you do is make things worse. Your motivation to know what is happening to him and find a remedy for his problem will be interpreted as if you are chasing and putting pressure on him. The jerk is such a fool that he cannot realize that you are looking for a solution to the evils that afflict him. Actually, the jerk is like a termite: he destroys, destroys and destroys.

Do not confuse isolation and rejection,

with the need for space.

If he does not want you to be by his side,

face it and move on.

Share your life with someone who does not want

any distance between you.

Characteristic # 30: **Affection: Where did it go?**

Characteristic # 30: **Affection: Where did it go?**

When you love, no limits or schedules are set. Love is expressed at every moment; true love can not be contained. That's the beauty of love, its spontaneity and naturalness. There is a passage in the Bible that I love because it fully defines what love—true love—is. 1 Corinthians 13:4-8 says: "Love is patient, love is kind. It does not envy, it does not boast, it is not proud. It does not dishonor others, it is not self-seeking, it is not easily angered, it keeps no record of wrongs. Love does not delight in evil but rejoices with the truth. It always protects, always trusts, always hopes, always perseveres. Love never fails. But where there are prophecies, they will cease; where there are tongues, they will be stilled; where there is knowledge, it will pass away."

It is wonderful to know that the love your partner gives you is true, that he suffers with you, that he is good and goes out of his way for you. He does not envy you, he does not compete; on the contrary he wants both of you to be equal. He does not boast or brag, because when someone loves you, does not feel superior to you. He does not do anything improper or lie to you. He does not slander you, cheat on you or hurt you; he is not unfaithful. He does not go around trying to please himself because his priority is not his own well-being, but the good of both of you as a couple. Not that there are no differences or misunderstandings; what it means is that despite moments of anger, love prevails and anger is not cause for a break up. The relationship is not volatile, ephemeral or temporary; on the contrary, it will grow deep roots.

Love will be tolerant and patient. It does not mean that you throw everything into oblivion, but that you learn from experience in a positive way. Love can see pain from a healthy and mature point of view. It does not rejoice in wrong against you and yours. It will make every effort to act honestly and in your favor. It delights itself in truth and honesty at all times, no matter the circumstances. It suffers everything; it suffers if you are not well, if something ails you or gets you down. It trusts and has no doubts about you (that's why jerks take us for idiots). It bears everything; this means that when we love, we try to save the relationship over and over again. When you love and you are loved, the relationship lasts for years; love matures and changes, but it is still love.

Jerks never learn or take part in this experience. On the contrary, they cry, go mute, ignore us, put us away, or worse still, consider us a piece of furniture in the house. Overnight, jerks isolate themselves and cease to show us the tiniest amount of love and affection. Then you wonder: what happened?

The answer is that jerks do not love; they become infatuated. Infatuation, according to the dictionary, is synonymous with acting. Acting is synonymous with pretending, creating or showing something that we are not. Acting is something fake; it does not come from a real feeling. Jerks may become infatuated with your physical appearance, your position, gestures, glances, caresses and the instantaneous emotions they experience when they are by your side, but this is not love.

The jerk makes himself and his partner think that what he feels is love, when he does not even know how to explain why he feels that he loves, or what awakened that feeling in him. The proof that jerks are infatuated and do not love, but rather pretend, act or fake their love for you, is evident in how easy it is for them to go from "love" to abusing, hurting, degrading and using you. They cheat on you and deprive you of your strength and security without taking responsibility for their actions or feeling remorse. It is evident when their rejection, manipulation, lies and unfair practices constantly undermine you. Jerks do not love or respect themselves, much less will they love and respect you.

Love does not leave room for doubt
it does not cripple you, or clip your wings.
Love is in constant growth
and its fruits are plentiful and sweet
in good times and bad times.

Characteristic # 31: **He prefers you mute!**

Characteristic # 31: **He prefers you mute!**

If after going twenty times around the house cleaning up his mess, your back is almost split into ten pieces, and if you do not even have the strength to take a good bath, maybe you'll want to complain; however, he will prefer you mute. After taking care of the kids for the whole weekend (even those from a previous partner), all of different ages and with different inclinations, and after taking them out to different places and dedicating yourself as a slave to caring for them, you might want to talk to him, however, he will prefer you mute. If after work he prefers to go out with his friends to have a few drinks while you are waiting with dinner ready and your best negligee on, when he finally decides to come home, if you ask him where he's been, he will prefer you mute. If you advise him to take care when coming home so late, because it's a long drive and fatigue combined with alcohol may cause an accident, but he still continues to do so deliberately, until one day it happens, he will prefer you mute. If he swears that he is faithful and never ever has cheated on you, but you find text messages and voicemail on his phone, if you even find pictures, and when he least expects, his sin is uncovered, he will prefer you mute. Your jerk will prefer you not to talk or say, "See? I told you!" "I warned you!" or "You should have listened to me!"

Jerks want to do things their way and not have anyone recriminating them. They do not want us pointing out their errors, much less they will acknowledge that we are right. We are mere decorative figures to them, which do not feel or suffer. They want us to act as if we do not hurt from their abusive acts. They think that we do not need to talk, vent or complain.

Jerks feel bored listening to our advice or warnings. It bothers them to answer our questions and receive our care. They interpret all our words as manipulation mechanisms. They compare us with their mothers, arguing that we nag them too much (the truth is that this should not be our role). How could we not do it when they behave like little children? If they were smarter, we would not have to walk behind them, fixing up everything they destroy along their way.

Jerks are like ignorant children; they have no common sense and have to be taken through everything, step by step. They act stubbornly and foolishly, on impulse. They do not wish to hear complaints either, but do everything possible to provoke them. Jerks do not want a woman; they want a doll with controls that they can turn on and off at will. Dolls can be displayed and manipulated without them saying a word. When jerks get tired, they toss them into the old toy box in case they need them later. The dolls endure all that the jerk tells them without complaining. (Remember, the jerks prefer them mute.) What the jerk does not realize is that dolls are hollow, empty, artificial and have no feelings or affection for him. Obviously, we are not dolls; we feel and suffer, and we deserve respect. For the jerk, this is incredibly impossible to accept.

We can not be tired, because our sacrifice is not seen as a job. Household chores or our daily duties will never have the pressure and importance of their jobs. Thus at the end of the day, only they are entitled to be tired, because the "hard work" is only done by them. They act as if we were looking at our faces in the mirror all day. Could it be that it is not enough to take care of the house, work, children and their pressure and nonsense?

Jerks believe that we do not have the right to ask for help, because we're supposed to be called on to handle everything about home, children and any situation that should come up. However, they are right there when there is a situation where they can look cooperative and loving, like heroes, responsible parents or understanding partners. Who do they think are fooling? Is it not them who are irritated when asked to fulfill these roles? Your jerk will prefer you mute, when he knows you are right. Your jerk will prefer you mute because when you speak out and ask for explanations, you expose his true self.

It turns out that you see yourself in this picture, dissatisfied with your relationship as a couple. You are practically tied up and unable to act and express what you feel and need. You cannot complain, suggest, comment, request or demand his attention and the love you deserve. Your partner turns out to be too busy, has no time for your "stupidities" and considers himself the most misunderstood. He does not communicate or share, and prefers to fill the house with people to avoid being alone with you. Without a doubt you feel like crying, but doing so will bring on his ironic stare, making you feel like a fool. The next morning, he wakes up, and you think, "He is sorry," and think that your tears have moved him. What a disappointment! To your surprise, he wakes you up to show you that the collar of his white shirt is dirty because you did not scrub it enough before throwing it in the washing machine.

You go after him around the house picking up his shoes, socks and all his crap. You wash and fold his clothes, sweep, mop, wash his dirty dishes and get not even a "thank you" in return. He just rewards your efforts with criticism and new demands.

It turns out that Mr. Misunderstood does not consider you good enough to make you the love of his life. Much less does he consider you his partner, and you will never be the ideal wife you dream about, although you can be an excellent maid. You will not say a word to aggravate the situation, and you will agree to all his requests, because you love him and want to make him happy. It is the perfect deal for him: you do not get a paycheck and you are a solution when he does not find someone else on the street to have sex with.

A serious and honest relationship
will not be a monologue.
On the contrary, it will be a constant dialogue,
open and frank between you.
It will be an open dialogue without limits
in which both of you can contribute ideas.

Characteristic # 32: **Sex! Not so frequent?**

Characteristic # 32: **Sex! Not so frequent?**

Sex: one of the great pleasures of life! While for some, sex is a taboo, a headache or a necessary evil, for others sex is a delight, the ultimate expression of passion and an outlet of lust. Some would categorize it as a source of total relaxation, which allows them to be transported to another level. Some consider it a torture lasting ten or fifteen minutes, when they have to pretend and hide many of their real and contradictory feelings.

Why should not we talk about sex? After all, we are a product of sex. Moreover, almost all of us take part in sex with more or less frequency. What a pity that not everyone enjoys it and makes the best of it!

Sex has been the cause of division among nations, church and families throughout history. However, it was established by God for mankind, for pleasure and as a method of reproduction. Sex is meant to be the greatest gift of your love for the one you love. It is supposed to be the climax of two people in love. Sex is the medium for the couple to maximize their love. Sex is just the beginning of many adventures together; it should never be the end. However, the jerks, and only the jerks, destroy this delicate altar of love.

Jerks crouch like wild animals, waiting for the right moment to devour their prey. Sometimes they hunt their prey, not because they're hungry, but to grope, frolic and show how many prey they are able to control and dominate at will. Like wild animals, they walk through life nibbling on their prey. They go from one victim to another just for pleasure, viciously. They release their animal instincts, leaving their prey seriously hurt, and then jump to pursue other prey, fleeing without the slightest sense of guilt. They are satisfied to leave behind many victims, injured and bleeding to death.

Jerks not only await the right moment to take advantage and gain sexual favors, but lose interest easily in the process. During the beginning of the relationship they have the urge to discover what you have between your legs, (as if they didn't know!). Jerks put pressure on us and insist on having us and devouring us in one fell swoop and in a hurry. Once they have what they want, they lose interest in us, and someone else takes our place. Such a sublime act is, to them, just a simple erection. Nothing but a hasty and plain ejaculation, done with urgency and out of curiosity. And we are climbing the walls! They turn sex into a reflection of their lives. They reflect what they have in their minds onto sex, captivated by their selfish self-love. They turn the act into what they are: empty and unscrupulous. They touch without feeling anything and look just for looking. Their minds are concentrated on friction and achieving their own pleasure. In their selfishness they do not take time for foreplay and the preparation of their partner. What in the beginning was a "debut" of cuddling, games, sweet words and erotic stimulation is now for them nothing more than taking your clothes off, giving you a cold kiss, penetrating and finishing. They butcher the act, the sensations and the desire. They inhibit you from practicing new caresses, postures and games.

This does not mean that for jerks sex has shifted to the background. On the contrary, sex remains a high priority in their lives, but not with you. One thing is certain and invariable in jerks: they love sex, but with multiple people. They love sex in different places, postures and forms, but with different people. It is likely you remember when your jerk made love to you everywhere: In the kitchen, on the beach, out on the deck and in many different ways, however, you notice that, for a while now, he cannot or will not do it so frequently. It is obvious that he is doing it with another person, or many others! He is bored! He lost interest! And you still tremble at the slightest touch!

Jerks enjoy having sex in different places. They like to try new things and satisfy themselves at will with other people, usually other than you. Note that I say people and not women, because some jerks experiment not only women but also with men. I guess you're thinking, "Impossible! My partner would never do that!" Think again! I am sorry to tell you, my friend, but you should not be so sure and should be more alert. You will be surprised at the things some people are capable of doing behind your back. Look at his attitude toward his friends when he thinks you are not looking. Look carefully at his reactions to unknown men, and you will see many signs—gestures and body movements that he might not commonly use.

Jerks usually appear tired and discouraged, and it even seems that they have sex with you almost forcefully. They pretend to be exhausted in order to avoid touching you or having sex with you. It is not that the others have something else between their legs different than what you have. It is simply that jerks prefer to try the forbidden, to pursue and seek out new sensations, rather than return to routine sex with you. Of course, they are unaware of those feelings because they visualize sex as a source of self-pleasure. In their exalted egotism, they view sex only as a service for self-pleasure. Jerks do not visualize sex as a gift for their partner of the best they have. Jerks can not transcend to this level in sex because they have nothing to give . . . they are dead inside.

Our body

is a most precious and sublime gift.

Give your body to him who

can appreciate it, cherish it and love it

with devotion and not to him who sees it as

a chunk of flesh

in which he can dump his lust.

Characteristic # 33: **Add insult to injury!**

Characteristic # 33: **Add insult to injury!**

Life next to a jerk is miserable. It is not enough that we endure insults, criticisms, comparisons, excuses, projections and uncertainties. After we bear the ghosts in his past, his withdrawal, the gag law imposed on us and the scarce sexual pleasure they give us, now we have to put up with his infidelity. Worse yet, they are unfaithful on multiple occasions, not with one but with several persons. They are unfaithful with people we know and even with those we have established friendships with or who are in some way linked to us. No, no, no! This is the tipping point! They go over the top and put an end to our patience.

Jerks are unfaithful with malice and forethought; they are cold, scheming and very calculating. They cheat, even knowing the consequences of their actions and realizing that many people will get hurt. This mess brings them more excitement and pleasure at the time of sex. The more complications and lies they carry on their chest, the more exciting and enjoyable cheating is for them.

When I uncovered my one-hundred-percent jerk's cheating, the first thing I noticed was that for several days his behavior was more distant than normal. He was constantly in a bad mood and was annoyed by any small detail. Everything seemed to displease him, and it looked like sometimes he wished that I was not there by his side. Even a simple remark made him greatly upset. He went to bed early and turned off his mobile phone, leaving it close to his nightstand. This suspicious behavior aroused doubts in me, so I waited until he was sound asleep. I took his phone and his car keys and went outside the apartment with great care not to wake him up. I locked myself inside the car, in the dark, and turned on his phone. I checked each of the outgoing and incoming calls besides the phone numbers stored in the contact list. I noticed that my name was stored with my full last name, as if a business relationship was all there was between us, not the kind of relationship couples have. I thought for a moment about stopping the search, but something inside me told me to continue. I proceeded to check his text messages, and he had messages from his ex-wife, his ex-girlfriend and other girls. Obviously not one was of the "Hello, how are you" kind. There were also messages sent to them by him. He told his ex-wife, "I love you." He told his former girlfriend that he wished he could have been with her in New York when we had been on that trip together, he and I, a few days before. He questioned the attitude of the other girls and told them he missed them or made them the same promises he had made to me.

While reading all these messages, my hands were shaking. I was furious and felt the urge to go into the bedroom and beat the crap out of him in bed, however, not with my hands, but with a baseball bat, and split his head. My mind was cloudy and I felt overwhelmed, not knowing if I should cry, kill him or run away. For a moment I wanted to get all my stuff out and never share a word with him, but I also had a desire for revenge.

In this situation of despair, I wanted to cry in anger, but because of the anger surge, my tears would not come. I called one of my best friends and told her what happened. I stayed up until 3:30 a.m. talking to her, but even when we said goodbye, the anger was still in me. I took a bath to try to come together, but to enter the bedroom and see him sleeping so calmly irritated me even more. Knowing he was lying to me with no remorse caused me greater anger. I got close to look at him, and I confess that I had to leave because I felt like killing him. Lying beside him made me feel nauseous and upset my stomach. The sheets, the bed, the room and breathing the same air as him caused me an unbearable need to throw up. I got up several times, went to the kitchen and drank some water, I went to the bathroom, I bathed again and again until it was almost 5:30 in the morning. All this until mental exhaustion overcame me. In the morning, he looked calm, as if he did not have any regrets. As I looked at him, so laid-back, I could not disguise the anger in me. When I do not like something or something is not right, I can barely pretend. I confronted him with my findings, but he was determined to deny everything at all costs. Like all jerks! They do things and then they do not have the guts to admit it!

Seeing himself caught in the evidence and without an exit, he hid behind my lack of respect in taking his phone without his consent. He had the nerve to say that the relationship had begun for him just a few days ago. Wow! What a jerk! That was his last ditch attempt at an excuse!

Jerks make up such vile, stupid and absurd excuses, that even they find them hard to believe. Their excuses are most stupid, without a starting point or foundation; they use the first thing that comes to their minds. In their lies, they contradict themselves over and over again, trying to justify their deeds.

195

Jerks make up the most absurd excuses to convince you that your doubts are imaginary and wrong. However, their actions only serve to prove we are right. You have seen enough evidence in text messages, pictures of other women, messages to their former partners, slips of paper with phone numbers in his wallet, women's clothes in his car and many other things, but he still denies it. It is then, that he starts asking us questions, to find out what is it and why we do not trust him. Knowing that you do not trust him as before bothers and annoys the jerk, because now he has to be more cautious.

Jerks do not want to accept when they are mistaken and have acted blatantly wrong. They tangle and try to twist facts to emerge unscathed from compromising events which they have caused. Anyway, there's nothing hidden under the sun. Jerks are miserable, and we do not have to endure them adding insult to injury. We are worth much more than this!

Unfaithfulness is a degrading and unexcused act.

It lacerates the lives of those who are deceived,

creating insecurity and despair.

Unfaithfulness does not have to be endured,

the decision is in your hands.

Characteristic # 34: **There is no forgiveness for our change**

Characteristic # 34: **There is no forgiveness for our change**

As if it wasn't enough, jerks are so thoughtless and inconsiderate that they do not accept changes in us. After stabbing us straight in the heart, they expect us to applaud their dirty tricks and pretend nothing happened.

Any woman who has gone through the difficult situation of infidelity knows that it disrupts many aspects of our being. Our privacy, intimacy and self-esteem are trespassed. Our integrity is overthrown, our trust is terminated and our self-respect is outraged. Infidelity grows all kinds of thoughts of revenge, hatred, betrayal and repudiation of the person who hurt us and who participated in doing us harm.

It is typical of jerks to demand and want to force us to forgive them immediately. They try to induce and precipitate a change in us, as if feelings had not been betrayed. The "slip" they had, or how many times they have done it, does not matter; jerks think they deserve our forgiveness. Even worse, they think they have the authority to force us to erase the facts from our memory and never mention them again. We all know that it will never be the same. Whatever the jerk does, if you stay by his side or decide to end the relationship, it will never, ever be the same.

Although you see twenty different psychologists and marriage counselors, it will not be the same, because the jerk has raped and invaded your feelings, your morals, your body, your self-respect and even your integrity. In all honesty, your jerk had to have remembered that you existed before committing infidelity. At least at some point he must have remembered your name, and if he still crossed that line, you should ask yourself: Does he really love me?

Cheating has many facets; it is not just about getting laid with someone. There are calls, sex games and other situations that show disrespect for you as a woman. It begins with flirting, a period of conquest and the exchange of conversations and calls. The jerk had to agree on the place, date and time of meeting, arrive, undress and consummate the act, and all this requires a process and many lies. If in all of these phases the jerk did not feel remorse for the pain he would cause you with his actions, and he felt no shame, no fear of being discovered, then he does not give a damn about you. Given this lack of respect toward you, the jerk is unforgivable. Worse, it is unforgivable that the jerk wants you to act as if nothing was happening. You are a human being, you have feelings, and you have every right in the world to change the way you are, feel and act, and even to refuse to be with this jerk.

Do not reproach yourself for his infidelity
nor blame for the failures your jerk committed.
Do not undermine your self-esteem
or cripple yourself mentally or physically.
You have to renew yourself, to assume a positive
self-healing attitude.
Find support, read and share your experiences.
You will surely feel better.

Characteristic # 35: **When they cry like little girls!**

Characteristic # 35: **When they cry like little girls!**

Interestingly, the complacency, selfishness and apparent self-sufficient attitude of jerks vanishes in an instant when you are packing your belongings to leave. I remember as if it was at this very moment when my jerk of an ex rushed over to me in tears. He hugged me and begged me not to leave. He cried as if he was being killed, and part of me wanted to laugh at how ridiculous he looked. I wondered, what is happening to him? Isn't this the same jerk that criticized me and compared me constantly? Where is the selfish jerk, my executioner, who replaced me with his friends and his job? Isn't this the jerk that was looking for excuses to end the relationship and said he needed space? Isn't it him that seemed to be bothered by my presence? Isn't he the jerk that had been unfaithful to me no matter how much I hurt? Why does he cry now? Is it guilt? Could it be that he does not want to lose me? Or is he simply afraid to be alone? Is he acknowledging that he has failed again because of his faults? Could he be pulling my leg again?

Jerks cry like little girls when they see the end coming for several reasons. First, they do not expect your firm and determined attitude. They are used to you silently putting up with humiliations, lies and deceit. They are surprised that you can not stand what they have been doing behind your back for so long. Second, they are afraid of losing something they took for granted, especially the sexual aspect. Third, but not less important, they are afraid of loneliness. Not only physical solitude, but also emotional loneliness and the need to feel needed by someone. Jerks can not stand being alone. Loneliness makes them feel insecure and reveals their greatest fears. Fourth, they are afraid of failure. Not because they wish everything between you to have a happy ending, but because others will see them as losers. They fear that others think they did not have the ability to sustain a lasting relationship and make a woman happy. Remember that jerks are dependent on appearances. Fifth, they fear memories. Although they deny it, at some point, when everything is over, jerks remember how they crippled and destroyed everything that you offered without reserve and with so much love.

When the jerks cry like little girls, it is not time to back down. Crying is one of their last moves—exactly the one you should ignore. Do not believe in their crocodile tears. Their tears and pleas are not an act of forgiveness and change; their tears are an act of desperation to maintain their appearance before others. The tears that are shed by the jerk serve to appeal to the nice feelings that he knows that you have and achieve his self-centered purpose of not feeling alone and unprotected. His tears reveal the fear of being exposed under the spotlight for his deceptions.

The tears of a jerk are not enough
to rebuild a broken heart,
to give you inner peace and give you back
your self-esteem and respect.
When you love you don't wait to reach
the end to cry and acknowledge mistakes.

Characteristic # 36: **They always promise to change . . . but never do!**

Characteristic # 36: **They always promise to change . . . but never do!**

If by chance you have not learned your lesson and you let yourself be convinced by his crocodile tears, I have to say that his acting will be temporary. I must also confess that I went through this. Promises were many but I never saw the changes. I think we all go through this at some point! Not because we are dumb as they think, but because we love them, and this is something they do not understand. They do not even love and respect themselves—the less will they be able to recognize true love! It sounds familiar to you: "Now, everything will change," "From now on, things will be different," "Now I'm going to work harder, and everything will be different," "Forgive me, I promise it will not happen again," and many things more. Is this true? These are the same promises they always make and never keep. What they call a second chance is for us the thousandth. There has been one too many; you lost track of how many, but the jerks conveniently forget. Even so, there you are again, going the extra mile.

Although this time you try to be a bit more cautious, deep inside you know you're giving an undeserved opportunity. Within, you still hope that one day all his promises come true. Although you have been lied to and cheated on many times, you still keep a pinch of hope. With your fallen and injured wings you try again. Seemingly the hurricane came to an end and calm arrived, but calm is in the eye of the storm—it is only an apparent calm.

The first few weeks, you see him willing and alert; he gets home early, and almost every night you have a 4th of July in your bed. Details that you thought were dead, resurface. He tries to regain the trust that you once had in him. He "works hard" to bring back to life the enthusiastic and expressive love that you had for him and that he had withered. You now agree over points of view which used to cause friction between both of you in the past, and you just couldn't get along. Apparently, now he is directed toward the same purpose as you. But the change in the hurricane's force is coming, because the jerk is concealing his true nature in order to keep you. You will see that after a few weeks he begins to go astray and seeks, like a wild animal, a way out of the "cage" that is trapping him, that is, you. As soon as he feels confident enough that you will not abandon him, he will return to his old ways.

Jerks are like wild animals; they cannot be tied to a relationship or to a woman, no matter how wonderful she is. If they are tied, they will live two lives, pretending to be what they are not until you uncover them. Sooner or later they break free of their cage. Life next to a jerk is made up of a host of broken promises, half-fulfilled promises, lies and rudeness. Jerks are not trustworthy, they are not men, and therefore they cannot fulfill their promises.

Jerks do not vindicate themselves.

They are meant to sink deeper every day

in their evil dealings.

But you do not have to go down the cliff with him.

There is always an opportunity to get afloat.

Characteristic # 37: **When it's all over . . . "It was your fault!"**

Characteristic # 37: **When it's all over . . . "It was your fault!"**

He hurt you again; he broke his promises, and now you feel betrayed once again. But now you do decide to break up with the jerk in your life. You have decided that the end has come; you feel strong and convinced. If you are no longer blindfolded, congratulations! I want to tell you that you've made the best decision of your life. Now that you have ended this unhealthy and exhausting relationship, you will notice that, without you realizing, the stagnation and lethargy that you were experiencing will end. Now you will feel liberated from the rushing and running around which you underwent to the please the jerk. You will free yourself of the feelings of guilt and inefficiency from not meeting his unrealistic expectations. Although you will have moments of weakness sometimes, the important thing is that you stay strong.

From now on you will have to be stronger, because your battle is not over yet. Your jerk will not just be sitting around. You will have to fight depression, your feelings of love, hate, anger and vengefulness. To make matters worse, you have to fight against those who will say you are to blame, but it is not impossible. At first you will be a bit confused to find yourself with free time of your own. You will be surprised that your friends find you different, happy, attractive and interesting. You will realize that it was you who was in a cage, not your jerk, and that you were wasting your life being with that good-for-nothing.

You have not even finished getting out of the relationship when your jerk starts to spread rumors. No matter what happened in your relationship with the jerk, no matter how much you gave to make the relationship work, you'll always be the culprit. You will hear many talking about the rumors and how he blames you for everything that happened. Remember, as I told you before, jerks project themselves and do not recognize their errors. Now you're part of their vicious circle. Remember when he said bad things about his former partners? Now he is doing that to you.

Why do jerks discredit us? As their plan for seducing and suffering did not work for them, their anger and true feelings come to light to hurt you, wound you and make you look bad before others. They remark and talk about what is not there to destroy the self-esteem you have left. It is typical of jerks that every time a relationship ends they point to their former partners as the culprits. As you already know jerks, this should prepare you and make you stronger, not destroy you.

Turn a deaf ear to all his remarks. Inside, you know all that you gave and sacrificed; you do not have to prove it to anyone. You have to stay calm, because you know you did your best. It does not matter what that jerk is saying out there and to whom; you can keep your chin up because even if you do not see it or believe it now, you came out victorious. You have many things that he does not have. You have the ability to love in an incredible way, which means you can restore yourself in a most amazing way. You have the courage to break this vicious circle, which is an amazing and admirable determination. You have learned from this experience and now you are stronger, more mature and invincible. By the way, eventually you'll see the jerk end up contradicting and exposing himself without you having to do anything to prove your innocence.

When someone blames you for his actions,

his weakness,

his immaturity and his poor ability

to learn from mistakes, become evident.

Do not fall before their negative remarks:

Show maturity, self-confidence, courage and

self-esteem. Reach higher!

Characteristic # 38: **His best allies!**

Characteristic # 38: **His best allies!**

It does not matter how much his family and friends liked you; at the moment of truth, you will shift to the background. The jerk in your life will acquit himself well, defended by his posse. His friends and relatives forget all the times you were the victim of his abuse, insults, dirty tricks and infidelities. It seems that they experience sudden amnesia and forget how much you gave and sacrificed for nothing. His friends and relatives separate from the feelings they said they had for you, and suddenly they mop the floor with you. To them, you're the bad one, and "their little son," their friend, their nephew or whatever is the holiest of all.

At first, his relatives will give you their condolences: "Oh, my gosh!"—to try to calm you down and make you understand that the poor guy "has been through very difficult situations." They will try to persuade you to think that the poor guy needs someone with lots of patience and tolerance to help relieve him of all the pain and trauma that lurks within him, because he has gone through so many difficult things. However, as soon as they notice that you are firm in your decision and have decided you will not take it anymore from your jerk, get ready: they will mop the floor with you. As the saying goes, "Like father, like son." Their best allies, their mothers, are extremely blind, so much that they cannot accept the fact that their children are not what they seem. Unfortunately, behind every big jerk there is a pandering mother. What about us? They forget our problems and issues. They conveniently forget that despite our pain and our difficult experiences, we gave their sons quality love. You simplified his life, treated him with tenderness, and you only got crumbs back from him. The mothers of jerks do not have the courage to accept that their sons are major league jerks.

We can not forget that no one is free from difficult situations. We all go through really painful moments and experiences at least once, but this does not give us the right to hurt others. Jerks have no right to take cover under the "Oh, my gosh!" their mothers love to say. His friends and relatives don't want to acknowledge that he can get out of this condition. They prefer the jerk to recover at the expense of your stability and emotional health. You know, it's more convenient! If he made up his mind, the jerk could seek professional counseling instead of going around crippling you.

Instead of hurting and using you, he should seek professional help. However, for jerks it is much more convenient to baby talk, play victims and put the blame on us. We have all suffered, but that does not mean we have a license to go around hurting others, so the jerks have no excuse. Their friends and family do not want to see or understand this reality. Years will pass, and they will continue to defend this jerk, the biggest jerk in the story of your life. To them, you will be the most "insensitive," who "wanted to control him," who "never understood his suffering" and who "came into his life at precisely the wrong moment." "She got into a relationship with him too fast, and everything was very rushed." "He needed more freedom, and she did not give it to him." "He needed time, and she rushed him." "She had to understand him more." "She lashed out at him." "She was to blame." "She had a very strong character." "She did not understand that all males have their lapses." "She did not understand that in a relationship one has to endure many things, even infidelities." "She did not understand that he needed help." "She was not thoughtful enough to soften his heart." "She . . ." "She . . ." "She . . ."

Well, let's change history. Imagine his mother in a relationship where her partner changes his mind quickly and is constantly criticizing her and finding fault in everything. Let us imagine that he does not include her in his decisions and activities, and she is the last thing is his busy schedule. In addition, let us imagine that her partner gives a lot of importance to what his friends say. On top of that, she has to endure constant infidelities. Will she put up with this? Will she accept the friends of her partner asking who she is every time they meet her, because he has so many girls at once that they can barely distinguish or recognize her? I'm pretty sure before reaching the middle of the list of situations that you have accepted from her jerk of a son, your ex-mother-in-law would have told her jerk to get lost. Then why should the situation be different when it comes to her jerk of a son?

Never judge a man until you've walked a mile in his shoes. His parents are blindfolded and are primarily responsible for the monster they have for a son. They will never blame their son for his actions. His friends will not face him either, because they consider your jerk as their idol. They criticize you behind your back, and when he gets a new partner, they will skin you alive. Faced with this situation, I recommend that you stay calm, because at the right time, God will bring everything to light. What they say about you so often will turn against them.

Your partner's parents are supposed to be like a second family for you, not executioners who harass you to cover-up the faults of their son. Reinforced by them, their jerk of a son will keep lurching. They will have many daughters-in-law, and only the one that puts up with the low blows of their son will be "perfect." You are worth more than this and deserve much more than these crumbs. You deserve to have a second family that values you, respects you and is fair with you.

Think about this carefully: as long as he has
family and friends who support his destructive
behavior,
he will keep being a jerk that does not feel
the slightest remorse.

Characteristic # 39: **He looks for you because he feels alone? Right!**

Characteristic # 39: **He looks for you because he feels alone? Right!**

Jerks, after their relationships have vanished, face loneliness and memories of what they had and ruined. Their loneliness, like all their crocodile tears and repentance, is superficial, vain and pure blackmail. Suddenly, you will receive calls from the jerk to explain how much he misses you. He will call to say how sad he feels, how he hasn't forgotten you, how much he wishes to see you again and be by your side and many other stupid things and lies. You will receive unexpected visits from the jerk. He will try to capture your attention again. After everything he did to you, how badly he treated you and what he said about you, how does he think you can believe his nonsense?

He will strive to make you believe he really needs you. He will begin the hunting game again. The sweet-voiced calls, text messages or flattering emails will not stop. Details like bouquets with little notes in them, and even an occasional invitation for dinner or to go out as before, will not cease. He will pretend before you and those that know you to show genuine repentance and a "sincere" desire to be by your side, or at least to remain friends. But what is really behind all this drama? What are the true intentions of the jerk? Will he return because he misses you, or because he needs to have sex with you? I can warn you, and I must tell you something that I'm totally sure of: the jerk is not returning because of love. If the jerk had really loved you, he would have shown you that when you were by his side. He did not have to wait for your departure to try to correct the situation.

The main reason for his comeback is because inside him, away from the bad influence of his friends, he acknowledges that by your side he had more than anyone has ever given him. He acknowledges his own evil in not appreciating the good experiences he had by your side. For this reason, upon looking at you again, his look saddens; he may bite or purse his lips in a gesture of shame, pretending perhaps.

Do not fall into the trap; it is not pity that you need. Similarly, the force of habit is not love. He can only offer sex—the same egocentric sex he offers everyone. The sexual pleasure he can give you is not what will heal your wounds. He cannot give you the love that you need, because he does not have it. Do not be fooled by the crumbs that jerks want to give you. The jerk is looking for you because loneliness confronts him with his existential void. What he has to offer is not enough. It was not good enough before and will not be now.

Force of habit neither is love
nor guarantees respect.
Habit is the cowardice of
not being able to face the world alone;
it is the codependency of
apparent stability and
fear of the unknown.

Characteristic # 40: **BONUS: He leaves you in pieces and he lives just as if nothing happened!**

Characteristic # 40: **BONUS: He leaves you in pieces and he lives just as if nothing happened!**

It's amazing the way jerks go out of your life undaunted and unharmed. Even more amazing yet is the jerks' ability to "rebuild" their lives and replace you. While you stay battered, in an absolute void, feeling helpless and miserable, the jerk seems to go on with his life as if nothing happened. You are left buried in a harmful depression, one which you think you will not be able to overcome. You cry until your eyes are swollen like a toad, your throat is dry and your nose looks like you have just been through a poorly done surgical procedure. And what for? What do you get in return?

Upon leaving the unhealthy relationship with a jerk you are left with the bitter taste of disappointment. You carry on your back the frustration of having given away all your strength, dreams and hopes. The impotence of seeing how everything has vanished and how it meant nothing at all for your jerk, haunts you. You experience anger because of what you gave, believed in and did not receive. You panic

Liz Aimeé Hernández

about your uncertain future; you feel a void that you don't know how to fill. The endless "whys" in your mind constantly overwhelm you, your memories disconcert you and your days feel incomplete and meaningless. You're so focused on the pain that you don't foresee an improvement. You often lose track of time. If you're doing your chores or you are working, you cannot concentrate, and while driving your car you forget where you are. You take the longest, busiest route, and do not use the shortcuts that you always used when you drove in a hurry trying to be the "Wonder Woman" and therefore sacrificing yourself for your jerk.

Leaving him has disrupted your life. It happened to you because you let your jerk be the center of your universe. Meanwhile, your jerk is neither flusters nor worries. The jerk recovered quickly from his apparent loneliness and is fresh and ready for a new conquest. He gets up every day feeling super macho. Knowing that you suffer because of him feeds his manhood and his eagerness to conquer new victims. He looks in the mirror, and no matter how ugly he is, he praises himself with the best compliments, admires himself and marvels at how great it is to be himself. He drenches himself in cologne (the most expensive and fashionable), fixes his hair and dresses for his new conquest, and does not think of you even for a moment. He thinks about all the new adventures that he will find and mockingly laughs at all who are in his past (including you). He knows that his former partners are still emotionally attached to him and feels victorious. His most evil purpose is to "win hearts" at will and then brag about it to his buddies. Every morning he prepares mentally, emotionally and physically to annihilate another new heart. Meanwhile, we foolishly look in the mirror every morning, criticize our hair, face, the extra pounds we have gained and how our clothes fit. We cannot find more faults in ourselves to point at. We are our own enemies. Every morning we prepare to be more miserable, prepare for someone to trample over us. We turn the jerks into winners with our defeatist attitude.

You lie in bed for hours without the spirit or the strength to go on with your life, however, your jerk wakes up in the morning like a spring. You can hardly take a bath and fix yourself up a little, but your jerk takes refreshing baths and dresses up with care and style. You choose the first 'rag' you find in your drawer to try to feel as comfortable as possible (though you look twenty pounds heavier), while your jerk will wear his best clothes to look more elegant and attractive than ever. You use a lot of ointments to relieve all the symptoms you have, take pills for your severe headaches and smell like a pharmacy, but your jerk is perfumed with his best cologne. You spend all day staring at your phone to see if you have missed a call from your jerk, while he receives calls from other girls and from his buddies, and plans new and fun outings. While you eat all the junk food you can find to fight the anxiety of not knowing why your jerk has not called, he will dine in a luxurious restaurant with his next victim.

Do not be a fool! Do not waste your days, your virtues, your talent and your life behind that jerk that just lost the most wonderful woman in the world: You! Get up, take a shower and dress up better than ever, for now you have the most important date in your life—with yourself. Fall in love with your virtues, talents and strengths without anyone having to mention them. Now is when you must indulge and pamper yourself the most. Someone once told me, "The worse you feel, the more you should dress up." This is very true; are you going to give that jerk the satisfaction of seeing you destroyed? No way! He has caused enough damage already! Go out, have fun, keep your mind busy, visit friends that you had neglected when you were just looking after the jerk in your life. Go out to watch a movie alone, enjoy the opportunity for a good meal or your favorite dessert. Yes, alone: it is delightful!

At first, you will feel weird, but then you will realize that it is the most important date you have ever had. Do not fall into not buying popcorn because you are alone! Indulge yourself, pamper yourself. A treat is not going to hurt you. Just don't go over the line; you do not want to lose your figure. Begin to fall in love with yourself again and learn to not rely on the company of someone to feel that you enjoy something. Buy yourself trendy clothes, dare to wear something different. Look for sexy underwear and wear it just for you. Show it off and dance wearing it in front of the mirror. You're not crazy; you will just starting to feel like a new woman. You will be surprised at the amazing results that these changes will have on your self-esteem!

Liz Aimeé Hernández

Never give someone more than

you would give to yourself.

Never give yourself the leftovers

that you would not give to others.

Characteristic # 41: **SUPER BONUS: In less than a month he is dating someone else!**

Characteristic # 41: **SUPER BONUS: In less than a month he is dating someone else!**

For the jerks, no matter how much they have humiliated and hurt you, is never enough. Their selfish and malicious nature always seeks to hit you with a final blow. Just to hurt you they hastily begin looking for another adventure. Do not be surprised if in less than a month they have another woman! In fact, even a month is a long time. We all know that in less than a week he would be spotted with somebody else.

And sex? Please! He has had sex with others long before you got out of his life. Moreover, perhaps in a month, what happened to me with my one-hundred-percent jerk (i.e. my ex), can happen to you. A month after breaking up with him, he invited me over to breakfast to confess that he had become a sperm donor for the fourth time. He could not even tell me who the other woman was because I knew her. Upon making some calculations with the pregnancy dates, it was obvious that he had been unfaithful and that my previous suspicions were true. He had been exposed.

Of course, after several months he claimed his fourth daughter was premature, to cover up his infidelity. I was not falling for that story! This cannot take you by surprise with jerks. You must be prepared to receive even worse news from them!

Do not let news like this one alter your system; on the contrary, let it give you great strength and a desire to excel! That jerk does not know what it means to love, and his life spins like a wheel again and again aimlessly. His new conquest might think she has won and feels privileged, but within weeks she will be ancient history, the business card that he will use to write down the number of his next victim. Do not get confused! Let nothing of what this jerk does steal your peace! Let your former jerk and her, celebrate now; you will see them fall later. Remember, he who laughs last, laughs best.

Perhaps at first you are not really sure of this, but soon you will see. Maybe your jerk and his followers look like everything is going very well for them, but someday, when you least expect it, you will get to know how life has taken care of the wrong he made you suffer.

Sometimes, months or even years pass before you see your ex-jerk fall and pay for what he has made you suffer. Just before I finished this book, I met a girl who happened to know my ex-hundred-percent-jerk. Through her I learned that he had started to pay for his misdeeds. As she told me, my ex-jerk met a young woman who was more street-savvy than him. In his quest to conquer her, he tried to surprise her with everything he could: an expensive ring, and believe it or not, even with a wedding. Incredibly enough, the jerk talked about marriage! Yes, because she was difficult to convince, or rather, very clever! It turns out that the jerk, in his attempt, planned a wedding in style, even with local artists. Just a few weeks before the wedding, she confessed to him that she could no longer be with him because he was not good enough for her. Since that day, the jerk has walked around with wounded pride, publicly carrying his shame. For the first time, the jerk received a taste of his own medicine. This jerk ended up becoming the laughing stock of all, and many who knew him were glad of his embarrassment. Moreover, according to her, more was happening to him, but she still had no details.

It is very true what they say: "What goes around comes around." You may have to wait several months or years, or you may never find out, but fate will ensure that your jerk pays for each of the wounds he caused you. As the Lord says in the Bible: "It is mine to avenge; I will repay," So, stay calm: The time will come for your jerk to pay, without you lifting a single finger.

The jerk will have women everywhere

but wherever he goes

he will find himself lonely and empty.

His happiness is only apparent.

Be prepared and be strong.

Soon you will see his wall collapsed.

Chapter 3: Why do jerks hurt us?

I often wondered why my former jerk-partners had hurt me so much, if I had loved them with all my heart and with all my strength. Why, if I had put forth all my effort, had I received so much indifference? Why, if I had given the best of me without reserve, had I been given only crumbs? Why had jerks sought the ideal opportunity to hurt me? What was it that made the jerks not satisfied with what I gave them? Why had jerks pretended to be what they were not? Why had I not seen the signs indicating that none of them was the right person? What was wrong with me? Why me? How do other women who have less beauty, talent, love to give, touch, sensitivity, intelligence and gifts have lasting relationships? Why, if I have positive qualities, am I criticized so much? Why, if I have everything a man could want, was I a victim of infidelity?

The questions were never ending and almost none had a logical answer. At first, I did nothing more than put the blame on myself and reproach myself over and over again. Each question revived the past and slowly drove deeper the daggers that the jerk had stuck in my heart. I was plunging into deep depression. I hurt more every day, trying to find a logical explanation for something that made no sense. I wanted to take the past in my hands, control it and change it. I yearned to find something to amend the past. I blamed myself for failures, as if I had been the only character in the story. I had forgotten that in a relationship, the two have a part. The fault was not all mine, but my question still remained unanswered: Why do jerks hurt us? After much tripping over the same stone without finding a satisfactory answer, I decided to thoroughly study the matter. Having spent many nights analyzing every detail, I finally found the answer.

The answer to this question is complex and involves different aspects, but it is clear, though sometimes difficult to accept. The answer is that jerks hurt us because we let them hurt us. With our attitude, we provide the perfect terrain for them to use and abuse us at will. I am going to show you which are some of these attitudes that we show others and that jerks take advantage of, to hurt us.

❖ **We have low self-esteem**
Self-esteem is a fine line between loving ourselves and feeling important. It is a fair and constructive vision for self-evaluation.

Self-esteem is the love and value that we give ourselves. Self-esteem involves loving and accepting ourselves as we are. Feeling entitled to live in a healthy, pleasant and positive environment and accepting the right and the freedom to be loved, appreciated and respected without having to do any sacrifices to earn it. Self-esteem is not feeling we have to change or do something big and wonderful to deserve to be loved.

Having a relationship with a jerk deeply disrupts the positive perception that we have of ourselves. It's terrifying to see how destructive words coming from a jerk become a powerful weapon against the one who believes in them.

There are people who since childhood have a tendency to suffer from low self-esteem. If these symptoms are not treated in time they may get worse during puberty or adulthood, as a person is faced with diverse experiences in life. Low self-esteem is the main cause of bad choices and hasty decisions. Low self-esteem leads to impotence in finding proper solutions for problems and makes us act against our goals, dreams and desires. Low self-esteem deteriorates our emotional, mental and physical health in a devastating way. Low self-esteem is one of the characteristics that jerks take into account when choosing their victims.

If you have a poor appreciation of yourself, the jerk can manipulate you at will, like a doll. You will be like a dry leaf that is blown by the wind. He will bring you up and let you fall at his convenience, stepping on top of you over and over again. Jerks easily detect women with low self-esteem. Your vulnerability and fragility give the jerk the perfect weapons to make you feel that without him you are nothing and you cannot function. With your poor self-esteem, you will believe everything the jerk tells you. Whatever the jerk wishes to change in you, he will. You will accept him and take the unpleasant way he treats you as the right thing to do. Because of your low self-esteem you will not feel entitled to demand better treatment or a better life.

Low self-esteem makes you fall into depression for wanting a better lifestyle without the courage to fight and demand what you want. Your low self-esteem is the starting point through which the jerk starts his move. This is the perfect opportunity for his misdeeds, to use you and leave you. This mental limitation is what the jerk wants so much for you to have for yourself—a mental limitation that you have imposed yourself before him, which will get worse as you spend more time beside him. It is a burden that is not ours, and someone made us believe it belonged to us.

Do you want others to value you? Are you tired of them using you at will as if you were the ultimate toy? Don't you wish never to be used and thrown away, wounded, into the old toy box? Dear friend, then you must begin loving, pampering and finding yourself. You have to start rebuilding your whole being.

Strengthen your self-esteem from the inside out. Many women, after a breakup, change their hair color or the style of clothes they wear, but this does not change what's inside them. You can change your image or what you wear, but if you do not change what's inside your head, you will fall into the same issues over and over again. You need to caress and be kind to yourself. You need to listen to your inner voice. You also need a lot of prayer.

God did not make a usual thing out of you: He made you in His own image, this is why you were able to go through the process of childhood which is so important. God made you to live, love and develop freely. He gave you free will, knowing that you have the ability to maintain a strong self-esteem and take control of your life. However, when going through the ordeals of life, we focus only on the damage that life left in us. We don't realize what we have overcome, managed and learned.

Each obstacle is a small step to strengthen our character and self-esteem, no matter how difficult. However, it is always seen by us as something negative, as a punishment from God or as a stumbling stone. We forget how we overcame previous obstacles and we get stuck thinking only of what we could have done better.

Low self-esteem is a limitation that we harbor within ourselves because of bad experiences, and jerks can perceive it and use it to their advantage. It is something you have to let go of if you want to be valued and achieve happiness. Self-esteem is not something that you can recover from one day to another; you have to work every day, every minute, every second to build it, restore it and maintain it.

You need a strong, confident and determined self-esteem to begin your path to happiness. To be able to enjoy life and savor every moment you need to love and nurture yourself. You need to control yourself, your actions and your feelings. You can not take control of your life if you turn a slight wind into a storm and you end up shattered. Be prepared to take the hit, recover and stand up stronger. Once you have beaten the storm, you must look back only to realize how much you have grown and matured, and not to reproach or criticize yourself for what you did not do. Rejoice because this storm did not beat you.

A strong self-esteem makes you see the bad experiences as opportunities. A strong and healthy self-esteem helps you get away from the jerks. It gives you the mental agility to identify them and not let them get close to hurt you. A stable self-esteem allows you to break free of the burdens left on you by the jerks and lets you overcome the wounds inflicted by them.

❖ **We make do**

As a result of low self-esteem we yield to the mistaken belief that we are not good, beautiful, nice and sensual enough for the jerk. We think that it is not important what we are but what others think we are. It may be that a past relationship, or maybe a friend or family member, has marked you. Maybe you did not realize that these people reflected their frustrations onto you, which now makes you fall easily for the jerks. Most likely, these people never met their goals, and like to infuse their fears in you, so you would never meet your goals, as well. These people are victims of a low self-esteem and they project it onto you.

This is why they make you believe that you're the weak one. They want you to feel and see yourself as insignificant. In this way, you are trapped in conformity, another key feature a jerk uses to hurt you. When I say that you "make do", I mainly mean in the emotional sense. You can be a successful professional, an entrepreneur and a determined fighter, but on an emotional level you have been left stagnant and subdued.

You are so hurt that when you encounter the first jerk, (aka "idiot"), you worship him as if you have hit the jackpot. Your need and desire of love is such that upon the first nice word he says to you, you become delusional and pour on all your virtues and then fall to the floor after not being valued as expected. You have so much eagerness within you for someone to value and love you, that you rush things and make mistakes over and over again. You want to feel alive and bury your past experiences with a new one, but you only manage to make another mistake.

The need to feel like a woman is very natural, but the rush to prove it is what leads you to choose another jerk. Do not settle for the first one that stands in front of you. Stop believing that you will not find someone better—this is not true. This negative way of thinking is a product of your low self-esteem, not of your true self. This is just what your jerk wants you to believe. When you meet a man (a man, I repeat, not a jerk), you limit yourself. You do not give yourself the opportunity to know someone better, and if you do, you feel afraid and insecure to be by his side, because you think you do not deserve him. You shrink and prefer to "make do" with the biggest jerk ever.

You need to learn to value yourself, knowing that you are important and have a lot to give. It is only in this way that you will be prepared to reject the crumbs that jerks give you and receive from the abundance of a genuine man. Abundance is not related only to money. When I speak of abundance I mean all aspects: love, respect, dignity, details, caresses, understanding, support, financial contribution, companionship, tenderness and many other details. In the end, you know better than anyone what you need, but you have to listen to your inner voice.

Do not settle for the first jerk that makes up stories, tells you sweet words or invites you for dinner. Think of all the virtues and qualities that you have, so as not to waste them on someone who does not deserve you. Think about how much it hurt in the past when a jerk used you and stripped you of your best to gain an advantage over you and then left cool as a cucumber. Think about how much it hurt when you did not give yourself time to analyze and know who was approaching you. You have shed many tears. Enough suffering for someone who does not deserve it! Think about this every time you hastily throw yourself into someone's arms. You do not want to go through a similar situation again! This is the time to change your life. It is time to not trip over the same stone. This is the time to vindicate your mistakes and not fall prey to unscrupulous jerks, to give yourself the opportunity of a change in attitude.

Think about all the opportunities you had to let go, and turn them into an encouragement to avoid falling into the same vicious circle. The image you have of yourself will make others see you as you think. The higher you look in your desires, the more you will get. It is not the time to stall and limit yourself: It's time to be free and enjoy all the things that are waiting for you!

❖ **We want to heal the wounds of others**
Jerks take advantage of our genuine interest in helping them. Since childhood we were given pots, brooms, dolls and baby bottles. We were

educated to serve and sacrifice ourselves to please others. We distort this service concept with the idea of postponing our needs to meet the needs and desires of others. We learned early to sacrifice our happiness and our physical and emotional health to heal the pain and trauma in others. This distorted idea was so well planted in our being that once we grow up it remains our only goal. We come to believe that the only thing we are good for is to help heal the wounds of others.

This is another quality that attracts jerks like a magnet. Our need to fix the hearts of others before fixing ours, causes us to be used again and again. Jerks appear hurt to get our attention and make us feel pity for them. We become the dustpan; we collect the trash that others have discarded: "He is going through a difficult process because his wife left him." Well, we have to look very closely at why she left him! Months later, when he has torn your heart, then you think, "Now I know why she left him; it is because he is a jerk!"

We mend, heal and correct ills they sought for themselves. We wrongly believe that upon helping them heal, they will value and love us, and they will stay with us forever. We submit to unnecessary martyrdom. We hear stories that were not for us to hear. We make their lives more enjoyable, providing them with the right weapons to rise, while they, in turn, end our lives. We are satisfied receiving pain, tears, suffering, shame and betrayal. We strive to vastly improve their lives so that others can enjoy them, improved.

This is why I invite you to stop doing it. Stop the eagerness to try to re-educate, guide and care. Teach, guide and take care of yourself first. Once you have done this, someone will come into your life who will not need to be re-educated and guided, but will be ready to offer you the best of himself. I once heard the phrase: "Never give a blank check" regarding my life. I must confess that I will never forget this phrase. However, in the past I forgot to use it in my life, and I paid with a lot of pain. In fact, now I visualize this phrase in a different way.

I do not view my life as a check but as a bank. The bank has an impressive architectural structure, is beautiful both in its exterior and interior. It has beautiful gardens in which many people delight while making transactions. Everything fits perfectly to the point that many people take ideas of its structure and its gardens to suit their own environment. Inside, the bank is even more impressive, and has sophisticated and luxurious decoration. Everything has a specific order.

The efficiency of this bank is well known, so many people want to work there, but only a select group is chosen to work in it. It is a bank that creates many assets daily and is invaluable. Do you think this bank should risk everything it has to devote itself to a single potential client? Should this bank bear the risk of bankruptcy and losing everything just for someone who has no assets in the bank? What do you think? I guess you answered no. Well this is exactly what we do when we devote our efforts, our gifts and our entire lives to please and heal the jerk beside us. Enough!

Stand up and take the place you deserve! Many (although you do not believe it or realize it because you're blinded by your jerk) would give everything they have, for you to look at them! They would go out of their way for your friendship at least, while you waste and reject everything for someone who only wants to lead you into an emotional, spiritual and physical downfall!

Later we will learn the reasons why jerks benefit from your gifts in order to survive. Meanwhile remember that you can overcome this; you can change this harmful pattern that you have allowed in your life so far. Dedicate yourself to spending time with people that nurture your spirit, that add assets to your life without causing more injuries. It is not your responsibility to heal the wounds of the jerks. Do not confuse love with the denial of your own existence by trying to heal others. There are psychologists to help them heal. Even psychologists are not supposed to heal the wounds of their partners, so why should you, who needs to heal too? You are not here for charity or free consultations. It is not your responsibility to solve anyone's life.

No matter how "hurt" the jerk is, it is not your responsibility to heal his wounds and leave your individuality to become his martyr. There are many therapies, treatments and trained professionals available to deal with these situations. They have already hurt you too much to carry this heavy burden alone. A broken heart needs to heal, not to mend another.

Heal yourself first, indulge and caress yourself tenderly. Never attack or cripple yourself. Beware; do not expose yourself to receive more injuries. Give special treatment to your mind, spirit and body. Give yourself time to heal completely. Worry about yourself first; you have long forgotten to do that by devoting yourself to healing wounds that are not yours.

❖ **We are too unsuspecting**

To make matters worse, and as if we had not already given too much, now we make the way too easy for jerks. We are very unsuspecting. When the jerk is late "because of work," we do not investigate. When the jerk misses an appointment because of a "family issue," we blindly take it as true. When his shirt is stained and he claims that it is ink, we lie to ourselves, even knowing that it is lipstick.

There are events that are obvious, and we turn our back on them. In the not so obvious (but doubtful) situations, we do not inquire or seek evidence. The same thing happens when the jerk comes to us and gives us his full "great guy" and "very gifted" performance; we do not corroborate the truth of it. By not doubting or being alert, we stop seeing that in reality his life is just a smoke screen. His life is nothing but lies, half truths, many exaggerations and fantasies. We swallow his lies and take for granted everything he tells us.

We cannot afford to be stupefied and lost in space. We need to listen and analyze everything. Observe everything: his actions, his friends, his favorite places, how he speaks to you and how he behaves. How does he address you, when he speaks? How does he call you? Investigate what motivates him to give you that nickname. Analyze his life, his habits and tastes, past experiences, and do not feel bad about it, since they also do the same without you noticing. You have to be vigilant at all times and everywhere. Do not assume you already know him and you know all about him and that you will live happily ever after. Remember, he could have the intention of becoming the next one to hurt you, and you have to take precautions to prevent this from happening to you again. Do not assume the "all is well" attitude. Rather assume the attitude that you do not know him; he is a stranger and you have to take care. You are worth a lot and deserve the very best. You have to be convinced of this—if you do not believe it, you'll always get less.

To keep the jerks away from your life, do a thorough research. No matter how long you take, do not rush. If your new prospect is really worth it and he values you, he will wait. Discover the true intentions of anyone who approaches you and shows you interest before making any decision compromising yourself. Learn all you can about him before getting involved and then hurt.

❖ **We do not check with God**

As I mentioned earlier in the book, our worst decisions are caused by us asking for guidance and support from human beings like us. We seek advice from people who are limited, stagnant or captive to their own problems and concerns. These are people who cannot cope with their lives, but try to solve ours: mortal beings, limited in space, time and knowledge. However, the source of all knowledge, which has no limit, is not consulted. We rule out the one who really knows all things. We rule out God.

If we at least would ask for some signs and left the decision up to God, we would make good choices, and therefore save ourselves from sadness and sorrow. God knows all things and knows us better than we know ourselves. God will let us know what suits us and what will harm us, if we put our faith and trust in Him. Only trusting Him will we find the peace we need, and avoid many unnecessary wounds. You don't need to belong to a particular religion; only talk to God as talking to a friend and you'll see huge changes in your life.

❖ **We assume that everyone has good intentions towards us**

This is a mistake we make over and over and over again. Since our intentions are good, we do not think that others think differently and may want to do us harm or benefit from us. This characteristic is related to being too credulous. We overlook that there are machinating minds because we live in a glass box that we believe unbreakable. This naivety makes us easy targets for jerks. They make their moves before our eyes and we cannot notice them, because we blindly believe their hoax. In addition to not taking the facts as they are (because we are so naive), we are also love-stupefied with them.

To take precautions against the jerks we have to start having a "criminal" and mischievous mind, like jerks. Only by knowing the enemy and thinking like the enemy can we prepare for combat. We must be more astute. Yes, very astute!

Women who have been successful in their relationships have been very, very astute. When we are getting to know the jerks we stop sharing and interacting with other people, especially people of the opposite sex, while the astute would think, "I'm only getting to know him, that is why I do not get involved or excited about him," "I do not trust him yet, perhaps it is something temporary, so I will keep going out with all my friends and I will continue my normal life."

❖ **We depend on the acceptance of others**
It is a fatal flaw to make decisions based on the acceptance and suggestions of others. You are smart enough to make your own decisions; if you weren't, you would not be reading this book. You do not need an outsider to master and take control of your life. You can listen and investigate, but do not listen and submit to everything people tell you. Be yourself. Think, analyze and make your own well-thought-out decisions.

Coldly analyze your situation, and whenever you make a decision, do it on behalf of and for your benefit and not for the benefit of the jerk.

❖ **Since we fear abandonment, we do not set our limits.**
If you have ignored embarrassing and uncomfortable situations just so your jerk does not go away, this is the first big mistake of your

life. Before starting any relationship, you have to know yourself well and definitely know what you will accept and what you will not.

When you are dating someone, do not break the rules you have established. Do not accept what you consider a lack of respect or something that is not within your parameters of tolerance and acceptance. Do not change and stop being who you are to please a jerk just to stop him from going away and leaving you for another woman. Jerks will go away, even though everything is perfect and despite all the indulgences you give them, it is their nature. Remember, he is not a man, he is a jerk; do not cede.

❖ **Jerks need a temporary driving force**
Jerks study their victims, use them for a while and then go away, but jerks are also used to not giving or receiving love. The jerk knows that although you are not perfect, you are wonderful, and he will want to enjoy your "gifts" to the fullest without getting involved, to get the most out of you. That is why he feigns, lies, pretends and exaggerates. He will blur your understanding to use you and leave your life in a flash. He needs your support and

emotional, physical and spiritual strength to recharge.

In short, jerks are less than nothing. Their exaggerations, lies, manipulations and hypocrisies are bigger that their integrity. They alone can not endure. They need to constantly steal identity, energy and driving force from someone that has its own light, like you. This is why he will hurt you. It is you who gives him courage and strength when he does not have them. When he is fearful and hesitant, you give him the necessary weapons, and as soon as he feels strong and "self-sufficient," he flees to squander what he obtained from you.

Jerks hurt us because they project their weaknesses, inefficiency and flaws onto our lives. They discharge their attitudes in us to weaken our minds and spirits. We believe in them, inject them with virtues to get their love and become their temporary driving forces. As a result, we end up exhausted by the effort. With their projection, jerks darken our minds so we focus our efforts on them, transferring our strengths to them while they give us their weaknesses. Great!

This is a chain −a chain that is very vicious, dangerous and damaging to our emotional health. Jerks make us depend on what they wish, want and crave. When their criticisms and demands make us weak and susceptible, they leave us. Jerks are highly insecure, but try to prove otherwise. They depend on the image of their friends and allies. Jerks listen and submit to their buddies, and so will have us do to them. He will subdue and dominate you.

Jerks need our encouragement and constant praise to keep functioning. They look for us as a refuge from their dreaded loneliness, but they easily find flaws in us and flee out of fear of commitment. If there is anything that jerks do not forgive, it is that you have discovered their true self. They do not forgive that you realize how great you are and how little he is; this destroys him emotionally and psychologically. Once you have used your strengths to fill his emptiness and he has something to present to others, he turns away and gives the fatal blow. When you let him see you fatally wounded, you give him the weapons to destroy you. He wants to see you destroyed so you can lack the courage and emotional and spiritual strength to reveal his true self to others. In this way he makes sure you remain silent, without "attacking" him. Jerks, not being able to carry the heavy burden of knowing that they did wrong, try to crush you and make you believe that you are worthless. They would rather have you surrender at their feet and obtain their victory.

Chapter 4: Kick him!

Maybe you wonder, why kick the jerk out of my life, and not just get him out? Great question! For women like us, who have loved and given too much, getting him out is not enough. After being with a jerk and enduring humiliation, comparisons, contempt, infidelity and more, getting him out is not enough. You have tried to get him out of your life before, and it has not worked. After everything that the jerk has done to you, you always look for excuses and false reasons to stay by his side, allowing him to keep hurting you even more. You have been too soft, generous and sweet with the jerk that has broken your heart hundreds of times. Every time the jerk inflicts a wound on you, you seek to remedy the situation, by hurting yourself with accusations, pushing yourself more, and changing even more to try to make the relationship work. No more! Stop whining, maiming, accusing and hurting yourself.

After all the suffering your jerk has caused you, the last thing you should do is continue mourning and hurting. I hope that after reading this book you have the knowledge to recognize when you have a jerk in front of you. I hope that this book has given you the necessary tools not only to know when you meet a jerk, but to flee immediately from his side and not repeat the same mistake that has hurt you before. I would like you to use the book as a reference, so every time someone comes into your life you review the characteristics of the jerks that I have described and stay alert. This does not mean you should stop living and enjoying your life, but if you want to be happy, you must be cautious and not take unnecessary risks by labeling everything as good and perfect.

Many times we let ourselves be carried away by new sensations and ignore the signs that pop up before us so clearly. We prefer to ignore the warning signs, to force ourselves to be in a relationship that we long for, but that does not really exist. At the end, we deeply regret not having taken note of these signs.

You do not have to hit bottom again. To be loved and valued, you do not have to be humiliated, abused or used. If you are aware of the signs, you will have the most powerful tool in your hands and will be in control of your life. Staying in control at all times, you will take charge of your feelings and actions, and will run on the right track in your new relationship. When I mention being in control, I mean that you will be conscious and alert at every step you take, without being moved as a leaf in the wind. You will have a say and you will value yourself.

If you fall into the same kind of unhealthy relationship with jerks over and over again, you will not be able to achieve any of this. Jerks, as you have learned throughout the book, just drain you and absorb all your energy and strength to feed themselves, just as parasites do. To finish healing and renewing yourself after you have survived your jerk, you must avoid falling back into the arms of another jerk. If you have already healed from your last one . . . congratulations!, but you cannot afford to be hurt and used again. Hasn't the recovery already cost you too many tears and too much suffering? Hasn't trying to recover your life been too hurtful and devastating?

It costs too much to get the pieces of your life in order and get up victorious after so much abuse. While trying to restore the damage that your jerk caused, analyze yourself: Will you allow yourself to be hurt again? Will you let yourself be utilized, compared, used and made fun of, as the jerks did to you in the past? Will you let them take the best from

Liz Aimeé Hernández

you and use it at will and without measure? I hope you have answered all these questions with a big and firm "NO." If your "no" was weak, I encourage you to read this book again and recall everything you have gone through.

Just close your eyes and allow yourself to "go back" to each of the events that hurt you most, not to reproach yourself, but to serve as a warning to flee from any guy showing signs of being a jerk. Value yourself! Value yourself! Value yourself! No one on earth, with the exception of God, can love and cherish you as you do yourself!

What a tragedy to be your own worst enemy and betrayer! Love, respect and forgive yourself! Only then will you be strong enough to stand firm and say "no" to any jerk coming in front of you. When you start breaking the sick routine of paying attention to jerks and stop letting them enter your life, you open the door for a real man to come into your life. You will leave the way uncluttered for a real man to nurture and love you. However, I must warn you that this will not happen overnight. My mother has told me many times that "the evil one usually strikes first" and this is very true. Life will test you. Not only once or twice: There will be several tests to prove if you are ready for something better.

272

When you love and value yourself and are not desperate to fall into another relationship, you will see great results. Once you have your life in your hands, in control, you will see great progress! When you have gotten rid of the jerks in your way and have learned from your past experiences, the man you have longed for, will come. That man will not be perfect, maybe he will not be your type, but best of all, he will not be a jerk. He will not humiliate you to stand up taller than you. He will not try to gain advantage, nor will he deceive you to meet his selfish objectives. He will not compare you, because he will value you for who you are, with your flaws and virtues. He will not be perfect, but he will be willing to make "adjustments" for the sake of having a successful life as a couple with you. I repeat again, he will not be perfect, but his virtues will outweigh his flaws. Perhaps he will snore or be a little disorganized; maybe he won't have the perfect body, but he will be kind, sweet, attentive and sincere. He will strive to improve those things that bother you. He will not hurt or diminish you; on the contrary, he will admire and appreciate your qualities.

The only way you can have a healthy and prosperous life will be by completely kicking out the jerks. Do not even bother listening to their nonsense or their stories. You do not have to be sweet, nor indulgent, with jerks. The only thing that jerks should receive from you is your indifference, followed by a categorical "NO!" and then, by the biggest kick in history!

Chapter 5: How to heal when a jerk has hurt us.

Each time I broke up with a jerk, I felt totally confused, hurt and devastated to continue. When I was hurt and desperate, I would look for some idea to arm myself with courage and rebuild my life again. I knew I would not find a magic potion to get rid of the pain and damage, but at least I wanted to have some realistic ideas about where to start.

I felt so empty and numb that it seemed almost impossible to think that there was a future for me. Nothing in my life had pleasure, smell or taste. It seemed that I wandered aimlessly on air. Mood swings were the norm. At that time what I needed and yearned for the most was to find alternatives and to emerge from the abyss in which I was submerged. But around me I just found generic answers: "Everything will be fine," "Don't worry," "People live through this," and "This will go away," amongst other things. You know! What everyone says when they really do not know what to say. None of these things was what I wanted to hear. I was too hurt, and needed something to relieve me deep inside. Those who gave me advice had not been through what I had. Nobody around me really knew the way I was feeling.

I desperately searched the bookstores for a book that would offer some advice that would take me out of the abyss where I was, but sadly I only found more of the same. Finding nothing to alleviate my deep wounds, I had to learn the hard way. I do not want you to go through the same, much less think that there is no hope.

Next, I offer you all the tools I used to heal when the jerks had hurt me. You can choose the ones you like to fit your lifestyle. However, if you combine them all, you will have better results. Start healing!

❖ **Rest**—Everyone insists that we must do something and never to fall off. Everyone advises that you should move, change jobs, change the color of your hair, go to a spa and look for a psychologist or counselor, among many other things. I advise you to do nothing of the above, especially for the first twenty-four hours. Let people at work know you need a day off for personal reasons. Then, turn off your mobile phone and stay home. Wait! I'm not saying you're going to lock yourself inside your home for weeks, forgetting that you have a life. No! Only those first twenty-four hours, remain quiet, in the safest and quietest place that you can find, which I hope can be your home. If not, try to find a peaceful place where you can relax and be safe. Maybe the beach or a resort.

I suppose you wonder: Why stay home for the first twenty-four hours? Call it a lapse of time to disconnect from everything. In these first twenty-four hours we, addicted to jerks, make the worst mistakes. In these hours we have a strong connection between the idea that everything is over and the idea that we are making the worst decision of our lives, which is not true. Since you will be wandering in your own space, I just don't want you to give anyone the pleasure of seeing you devastated.

During this time it is vital that you stay alone, not to hurt yourself or start calling the jerk, but to rest. Take the opportunity to rest, so your body gets in tune with your mind, and you can be able to think clearly and recover the strength to face your new life. If you prefer, you can notify a family member or close friend (one you trust) that you will be resting and need to be alone without being interrupted. They will surely understand!

Before you go to sleep, prepare a warm bath or stay a long time under the shower, relaxing and calming down. Do not think of anything or anyone! Relax, trying to concentrate and listen to your heartbeat and your breathing. Silently, close your eyes and enjoy the warm water touching your skin. It is better if you use scents in the bathroom or in the water or a scented soap to relax. Do not rush when bathing; do not leave the shower until you feel quite calm, so you can prepare your body and your mind to rest.

Upon exiting the shower, apply a smooth and relaxing scented cream. Use the most comfortable sleepwear that you have. Then go straight to the kitchen and fix yourself some tea or a hot comforting drink, or take a natural supplement to help you relax. If you do not like tea, drink plenty of water to hydrate. Do not take sleeping pills! Now . . . go rest!

❖ **Cry and throw a tantrum!**—Those of us that have gone through the experience of kicking out jerks know that a warm bath is not enough to feel totally fine. After those first twenty-four hours, you will still be dazed and disoriented. The need to cry will come to you suddenly. This is when many people will say that you should not cry, and other nonsense. My advice is to cry and throw a tantrum! If you have to get into the shower again, or lock yourself in your room to cry and shout, do it. Nothing is more comforting than to release repressed feelings.

Wounds of the soul need to be treated as wounds in the skin. When we suffer an injury and are bleeding, it is necessary to clean it and remove any unwanted particle that may be there. After it is clean we need to apply pressure to stop the bleeding. A wound cannot heal if it is not clean and if it was not given proper care. There is nothing wrong with crying and letting the pain out; it is a very normal and necessary process for healing.

❖ **Talk, talk, talk!**—Externalizing what you feel is an essential part of the healing process. If you have a friend or relative that you trust fully, explain to him or her what you are going through. If you can, ask that person to support you. Let him or her know that all you need is someone who is willing to listen as often as necessary, even if he or she does not say a word. Beware! Do not pick someone who is going through a similar or worse situation. You need someone who has healed, who will not use you to vent their frustrations and project their anxieties. Be selective! If you do not trust anyone to listen openly without judging, criticizing or forcing you to heal, then I suggest you write down everything you feel. When you have put everything you feel on paper, shred it and get rid of it. You can buy a pet or a stuffed animal and talk to it as if it was listening to you. You can seek a professional counselor or a minister who is willing to listen. Now, I'm not saying you're going to stay like this for a lifetime! Do not think that I am crazy, either! You have to externalize your feelings over and over again, and the best way is to talk, talk, and talk.

❖ **Read devotional books**—Every morning, after you wake up, read at least a fragment of a devotional book of your choice, or perhaps the Bible if you like. Underline the portions that you find comforting. Copy the words that give you more encouragement and inspiration. Paste them in a visible place that you frequently visit. You can have some on the door of your fridge, on your computer monitor, on the door of your room or office and everywhere you think necessary.

When I broke up with my hundred-percent jerk of an ex, I was determined to not let anyone else hurt me again. I had decided to restore my life completely. However, to do so, I needed so many encouraging and reinforcing words. I had positive messages and Bible passages in all my most visited places, even in my purse. To heal, you need to customize healing strategies and use your wits to match your lifestyle and needs.

❖ **Analyze your changes**—The healing process is a slow process. Significant changes do not show overnight, but during the process you can see small changes that indicate that you are on the right track. After breaking up with your jerk, it is normal to feel a total devastation, and trapped in a dark storm because the jerk drained you. However, if you analyze your different moods, you will notice that your mind and body are responding positively to your recovery. As I mentioned earlier, do not expect big changes instantly; small changes will lead you to a great transformation. To understand the small but firm steps you are taking, you need time alone and in silence. You can visit a park, sit facing the sea, a river or a lake or simply sit back for a while in your bed. With your eyes closed, analyze objectively from the first twenty-four hours until today. You could even write down what you have felt from day one and watch your progress. Compare both situations, not to criticize yourself and mourn, but to help yourself realize how you have improved.

Perhaps in those first twenty-four hours you were thinking that the sky had fallen over you, and perhaps even today you still do not feel fully recovered, but at least you are not floating vaguely in the air. The fact of recovering your orientation and feeling less stunned are good signs. These show that you are aware of what happened and are ready to fight. They do not mean total healing, but they are the necessary ingredients in a new approach in your life.

❖ **Do something you have not done before—** During the time you take to think, identify something you have not done before and would like to achieve. Maybe traveling, starting a new business, collecting something, studying or enrolling into an organization, amongst other things. The list can be endless; what matters is that you look for achievable activities, so you do not get frustrated. Put a title on your list and divide it into short, medium and long-term plans. For each of them, write the steps you have to take to achieve them. For example, if you want to travel, set your destination, do a little research and estimate how much money you will need. Determine an approximate time-frame and start a daily savings program to meet your goal. Do not try to make big moves, because you're in a healing process in which you are still very sensitive and fragile. If you hurry to make great strides, you can get frustrated, make bad decisions and even worsen your emotional state even more.

Every step you take must be well studied, well pondered. The most important thing is that you're being proactive. You are taking control of your life again, but above all, preparing for a more stable future, maturing and gradually healing. Now that you have new plans to take care of, time will pass almost without you realizing it!

❖ **Change your phone number**—With a good rest, a good devotional and new plans for your life, the only thing that does not fit is the directory of ghosts that you have in your phone. Erasing your jerk's numbers is not enough. You must change your phone number! Every time I was in the healing process, I was interrupted by a call or message from my ex-jerk and his ghosts. This lack of concentration caused delays in my process, since negative thoughts and memories returned.

You need to change your phone number, even your e-mail account. Do not store any of the numbers of your jerk, so you are not tempted to fall at his feet calling or leaving messages. The more disconnected you are from everything that happened with your jerk, the more ideas and energy you will have to concentrate on your new projects.

- ❖ **Reorganize and redecorate your home**—Now that you have left your jerk in the past and have started to work on your new projects, you need a friendly, relaxing and quiet atmosphere that inspires new ideas. To redecorate your home, you don't need to invest large sums of money or buy new things. You can change the place or position of the motifs and decorations in your home. Exchange the accessories you use in one room with others. If you have the money, you can change the color of some of the walls or your bed sheets. However, do not try to make all the changes at once. Tackle one room at a time.

Prepare the rooms to your liking and remove from them any memory of your jerk. You can even start by redecorating the place that your jerk enjoyed the most. (It will be fun to change everything he loved!) Opt for bright and cheerful colors. Allow natural light to enter the rooms and air to circulate constantly. For a positive energy flow, keep the room organized and add plants. Enable spaces according to your needs, your lifestyle and your new projects.

❖ **Visit a church**—How can we heal if we do not have the Doctor of doctors? No permanent healing process exists if God is not included in our plans! As I said before, you don't need to belong to any church or be a religious fanatic, but it would be good to hear words of encouragement with a spiritual focus. Be selective; do not choose a church that overwhelms you and weighs you down with its rules, taboos and prohibitions. Choose a church that gives you the tools to aid in your healing.

You can inquire amongst friends who attend church, but only by visiting them will you know if they have what you need. Listen to your instincts! Do not settle for the first church you find, and if anything makes you uncomfortable or does not feel right, do not just make do!

❖ **Exercise and eat well!**—Since you are now organized, have new purposes and intend to achieve spiritual healing, you cannot neglect your diet. You have several things demanding a lot of energy from you. These variables, including kicking your jerk out, finding yourself, setting your new goals and restoring yourself, require you to be strong and healthy.

Exercise, besides giving you a beautiful figure and a slender body, is an excellent way to release all those negative charges that had accumulated with the jerk in your life. Exercise promotes the proper functioning of your body and eliminates toxins—just what you need to stay awake, alert and focused and get your self-esteem back.

In combination with exercise, a balanced diet will give you the strength and resources to beautify yourself from the inside out and create permanent changes in your new image. After all, that is what we want—permanent changes! This does not mean you now have to run six miles or practice bodybuilding! However, it would be convenient to go out for a thirty minute walk at least three times a week or to attend a gym.

Try to eliminate fats, caffeine, soft drinks, tobacco and strong drinks, and instead drink eight glasses of water or more a day, take larger servings of fruit, vegetables and foods rich in fiber.

Stay away from expensive memberships and crash diets. Take care at first to only use exercise as a means of relaxation and release of suppressed feelings. Later, when your body gets used to the routine and feels freer, you can establish more demanding goals. Exercise will be a good complement and excellent support to your healing plan!

❖ **Renew your appearance**—Now that you have included in your life all the necessary elements to heal as you should this is, starting from the inside, you can determine more clearly what details you would like to improve in your appearance. As I mentioned earlier, first you must accept yourself as you are. Do not push yourself to make changes that are not real. Many times, we don't need to make major changes. Sometimes a more youthful hair style, a brighter hair color or fresher makeup is enough to transform our image. Before making an image change you must be sure of what you want. Seek the opinion of different professionals. Do not try to do everything at once! Ask around so the changes you make brighten your face and highlight your natural attributes. Choose changes that are within your budget so you can follow up appropriately and maintain your new image. After some changes you will feel more comfortable with your looks, and you will project more self-confidence.

❖ **Renew your wardrobe**—A makeover involves reviewing your wardrobe! To be able to project your new image, you don't need to discard all your clothes or spend a lot of money. Simply make different combinations with the clothes you already have. Take the clothes in your closet and place them on your bed. I recommend you schedule a few hours just for this. Use underwear that favors your figure and start trying combinations. Have pencil and paper ready to keep track of the garments that you need to buy for the combinations you are trying, including the accessories you need and the new underwear. Adopt the good habit of matching your underwear with your exterior clothes. Wear delicate lingerie; you will feel better and more beautiful! Intimate, delicate and very feminine underwear must be part of your wardrobe, even if you use it just for yourself. Use it every day! Yes, just for you! Some women have the bad habit of using sensual and delicate clothes only when they have sex. Wrong! You have to feel sensual, delicate and beautiful for yourself every day first! Do not forget to include sleepwear, shoes and handbags in your list! You do not need too much –only key pieces, which you can use with many clothes.

❖ **Go shopping**—After discovering exactly what you need comes the time to go shopping. First, visit several places to compare styles, prices and textures. Do not buy the first thing you see! Stay away from fads that do not suit you! Do not buy things just to have the latest fashion. Do not buy clothes that you need to alter or adjust. Try to stick to the list you have already prepared. In this way you will save time and money. Staying focused on the items you have identified, instead of mixing things impromptu, will create the image you so much desire.

❖ **Pamper yourself**—Now that you have already made so many efforts and are doing the best you can to heal, you must give yourself a reward. You, better than anyone, know what things make you feel rewarded. Maybe a facial, an ice cream, or a blouse. It depends on your personality and tastes. Identify small rewards that do not affect your budget, let alone your figure. Reward yourself on some special occasion. It can be on the day when you feel more tense or weak. Or perhaps the day you accomplish one of your new projects.

❖ **Go out on a date with yourself**—Finally (but certainly not least important), periodically, take a scented bath, wear your sexiest clothes and dress up for the most important date in your life: A date with yourself! Choose a restaurant, a movie theater or other place. Bars, clubs, or anything similar are not allowed! Remember, it is a date! Do not be afraid to go into the place alone. Order your favorite drink and an appetizer, and remember . . . you are not in a hurry. Maybe at first you will feel odd or you will notice that everyone looks at you in a strange way, but this is part of the process of getting used to having a life of your own. Enjoy every moment. While waiting for your food, close your eyes and enjoy the moment. Do not devour the food; enjoy every bite. Fall in love with yourself and the feeling of freedom. Be passionate in your independence. Get excited to know yourself. Wrap yourself in recovery day after day and compliment yourself. You'll see that soon you will get used to this. Then you will not be able to stop booking dates with yourself in your daily planner.

Each of these tips helped me survive the damage from all the jerks that passed through my life. Surviving the wounds left by jerks is not easy, but it is not impossible either. The hardest job was breaking the habit of being a prey to the jerks, but I hope you have learned how to not become a victim of any jerk again. You can use and repeat these tips as much as you need; however, the decision is in your hands.

The price to pay for being with a jerk is too high, but you have the power to control this situation in your hands. Stand firm, and do not back down even for a second! Go ahead . . . Kick the jerk out of your life . . . forever!